D [illegible] t

Edited by Na[illegible] [illegible]cember 2012

The Bible Reading Fellowship
15 The Chambers, Vineyard, Abingdon OX14 3FE
Tel: 01865 319700; Fax: 01865 319701
E-mail: enquiries@brf.org.uk; Website: www.brf.org.uk

ISBN 978 1 84101 673 3

Distributed in Australia by Mediacom Education Inc., PO Box 610, Unley, SA 5061.
Tel: 1800 811 311; Fax: 08 8297 8719;
E-mail: admin@mediacom.org.au
Available also from all good Christian bookshops in Australia.
For individual and group subscriptions in Australia:
Mrs Rosemary Morrall, PO Box W35, Wanniassa, ACT 2903.

Distributed in New Zealand by Scripture Union Wholesale, PO Box 760, Wellington
Tel: 04 385 0421; Fax: 04 384 3990; E-mail: suwholesale@clear.net.nz

Publications distributed to more than 60 countries

Acknowledgments

Printed in Singapore by Craft Print International Ltd

Suggestions for using *New Daylight*

Find a regular time and place, if possible, where you can read and pray undisturbed. Before you begin, take time to be still and perhaps use the BRF prayer. Then read the Bible passage slowly (try reading it aloud if you find it over-familiar), followed by the comment. You can also use *New Daylight* for group study and discussion, if you prefer.

The prayer or point for reflection can be a starting point for your own meditation and prayer. Many people like to keep a journal to record their thoughts about a Bible passage and items for prayer. In *New Daylight* we also note the Sundays and some special festivals from the Church calendar, to keep in step with the Christian year.

New Daylight and the Bible

New Daylight contributors use a range of Bible versions, and you will find a list of the versions used opposite, on page 2. You are welcome to use your own preferred version alongside the passage printed in the notes, and this can be particularly helpful if the Bible text has been abridged.

New Daylight affirms that the whole of the Bible is God's revelation to us, and we should read, reflect on and learn from every part of both Old and New Testaments. Usually the printed comment presents a straightforward 'thought for the day', but sometimes it may also raise questions rather than simply providing answers, as we wrestle with some of the more difficult passages of Scripture.

New Daylight *is also available in a deluxe edition (larger format). Check out your local Christian bookshop or contact the BRF office, who can also give more details about a cassette version for the visually impaired. For a Braille edition, contact St John's Guild, 8 St Raphael's Court, Avenue Road, St Albans, AL1 3EH.*

Writers in this issue

Andrew John has been the Bishop of Bangor since 2008, having previously served all his ministry in the Diocese of St Davids. He is married to Caroline, who is also a deacon in the Church in Wales.

Rodney Holder is Course Director of the Faraday Institute for Science and Religion, St Edmund's College, Cambridge. His latest book is *The Heavens Declare: Natural Theology and the Legacy of Karl Barth*.

Helen Julian CSF has written several books for BRF, most recently *The Road to Emmaus*. She is an Anglican Franciscan sister, and presently serves her community as Minister General.

Michael Mitton is a freelance writer, speaker and consultant and the Fresh Expressions Adviser for the Derby Diocese. He is also an honorary Canon of Derby Cathedral. He is the author of *Dreaming of Home* (BRF, 2012).

Heather Fenton has recently taken retirement from parish ministry but continues with work connected with publishing. She had also been involved in running a small retreat house in rural north Wales.

Veronica Zundel is an Oxford graduate, writer and journalist. She lives with her husband and son in North London, where they belong to the Mennonite Church.

Naomi Starkey is a Commissioning Editor for BRF and edits and writes for *New Daylight* Bible reading notes. She has also written *Good Enough Mother* (BRF, 2009).

Amy Boucher Pye is an American who has lived in the UK for over a decade. She makes her home in North London with her husband and young family and enjoys writing for Christian periodicals.

Stephen Rand is a writer and speaker who in recent years has shared his time between Jubilee Debt Campaign, persecuted church charity Open Doors and Mainstream—a Baptist church leaders network.

Steve Aisthorpe is a Development Officer for the Church of Scotland, encouraging mission and discipleship throughout the Highlands and Islands.

Maggi Dawn is an author and theologian, currently based at Yale University, where she is Dean of Marquand Chapel and Associate Professor of Theology and Literature in the Divinity School.

Naomi Starkey writes...

I was reading a book on biblical criticism the other day (editors need to keep on their toes, theologically speaking!) and was struck by the phrase 'a responsible reading'. The author of the book was reflecting on the importance of learning to read the Bible 'responsibly'—in other words, taking into account the original context, audience, what scholars have said about it, and so on.

It's a helpful concept because it reminds us of the significance of Bible reading and the priority we should place on doing it well, because the way we interpret what we read has implications not only for ourselves but for our friends, family, church and the wider community.

My hope is that *New Daylight* offers encouragement to develop and practise this habit of responsible reading, although there is, of course, a limit to what we can fit into a 'page a day' format. While we cannot necessarily provide a definitive pronouncement on a given topic, the notes can provide a starting point for further thought, discussion and study, especially if the passage covered involves complex or challenging ideas.

With this in mind, I am pleased to include in this issue readings on 'Our Creator God' by Rodney Holder, Course Director of the Faraday Institute. This is a Christian-based academic research organisation at St Edmund's College, Cambridge, which also runs courses, seminars and conferences to educate people about religion and science. I appreciated his reminder (on 10 September) that even early church theologians, such as Augustine, did not read Genesis 1 literally. As he puts it, 'It is a literary masterpiece, describing creation from a theological perspective.'

It is also good to feature another set of readings in our 'Bible stories rediscovered' series, with Stephen Rand writing on Joshua and the fall of Jericho. While the story is popular in children's story Bibles and Sunday school classes, a 'responsible reading' of the text will inevitably raise some potentially awkward questions as well as providing answers.

Finally, I would like to say a special good bye and thank you to John Proctor, who has written for *New Daylight* for a number of years. It has been good to have his contributions in the notes and we wish him all the best in his future ministry.

The BRF Prayer

Almighty God,

you have taught us that your word is a lamp for our feet
and a light for our path. Help us, and all who prayerfully
read your word, to deepen our fellowship with you
and with each other through your love.
And in so doing may we come to know you more fully,
love you more truly, and follow more faithfully
in the steps of your son Jesus Christ, who lives and reigns
with you and the Holy Spirit, one God for evermore.

Amen

Titus

I want to make it clear that I am not a great fan of Bonnie Tyler's 1984 song 'Holding on for a hero'! The song seems to paint a picture of the archetypal warrior who has biceps as big as medicine balls and a torso constructed by the very latest CGI technology. The reality is that what is truly heroic is less spectacular than the song I have just referred to—and the Bible has a great deal to say about the things that really count, the qualities and attitudes which are truly desirable and worthy.

At the heart of Christian life is the call to follow Jesus and become a disciple. This takes us beyond statements of belief to matters such as lifestyle and behaviour. The letter to Titus is one of what are called 'The Pastorals' and, like the other Pastorals, it is concerned with the quality of Christian living. It was written following Paul and Titus' evangelisation of Crete, when Titus was left there to complete the establishment of sound Christian communities.

Although it is not easy to fit this letter into the events described in Acts, there are probably gaps in the account where this letter should be inserted. The context is, of course, less significant than the content. The value of nurturing healthy churches shows how Paul could see the strategic importance of good leadership and those qualities that are quite different from those in Bonnie Tyler's song. That is, leadership would be tested and tried and need to be well founded if it was to succeed.

In this letter we see how Paul deals with some very practical matters, such as relationships in the family, commitment to public life and the importance of paying attention to our own commitment to Christ. Underpinning all that, Paul says, is a clear understanding of the God who is revealed in Jesus Christ, whose death and resurrection has brought 'the hope of eternal life' (3:7). Although the letter is directed to a leader called to make leaders, its message has wider significance because of the way faith and living are held together. For this reason, it has enduring appeal and importance for others—for you and for me.

Andrew John

TITUS 1:1–4 (TNIV)

The privilege of knowing God

> Paul, a servant of God and an apostle of Jesus Christ to further the faith of God's elect and their knowledge of the truth that leads to godliness—in the hope of eternal life, which God, who does not lie, promised before the beginning of time, and which now at his appointed season he has brought to light through the preaching entrusted to me by the command of God our Saviour. To Titus, my true son in our common faith: Grace and peace from God the Father and Christ Jesus our Saviour.

Some people think the origin of shaking hands has a less generous history than we might assume—that it involves swords and a clear line of sight so that the physical contact does not mask something rather nastier than a hand! Nothing could be further from the greeting Paul brings to his 'true child' Titus, who, with Paul, shares a common faith. It is warm-hearted and founded on the grace they have come to share. Paul bases this close relationship on three truths. First, on the truth of God in whom grace and peace are found (v. 4). Second, on the service Paul renders as a servant of God and an apostle of Jesus Christ (v. 1). Third, in the way God calls servants such as Paul for the sake of others: he describes Christians as God's elect (v. 1). They are the very ones for whom Paul's life and ministry now exists.

What do these words offer us today? Let us consider two thoughts: first, that the most important of all relationships is with God. Nothing could surpass this pressing and life-giving relationship that is possible in Jesus. Do you feel that you have such a relationship with God? Second, our relationship with other Christians is vital because that, too, is founded on God's grace. Those who belong to God are now our brothers and sisters and, with us, part of a new family.

Prayer

Heavenly Father, we thank you for Paul, who made connections between what he knew to be true and what this meant for his life. Give us new eyes to do the same and respond for the sake of Jesus Christ. Amen

ANDREW JOHN

Titus 1:5–6, 9 (TNIV)

Even better than the real thing

The reason I left you in Crete was that you might put in order what was left unfinished and appoint elders in every town, as I directed you. An elder must be blameless, faithful to his wife, a man whose children believe and are not open to the charge of being wild and disobedient... He must hold firmly to the trustworthy message as it has been taught, so that he can encourage others by sound doctrine and refute those who oppose it.

Many years ago I was given a present following my grandmother's visit abroad—a Rolex watch! A Rolex watch that cost all of $2.50 from a side street salesman.

Sometimes the imitation is very inferior to the real thing. In today's reading, Paul describes the qualities needed for authentic ministry and shows how personal integrity is crucial for any such responsibility. He begins with a reminder of how Titus was charged with appointing leaders 'in every town' (v. 5). He lists, negatively (vv. 6–7), what must be avoided and, positively, what must be nurtured (vv. 8–9). To begin with, a Christian life and faith contains boundaries. There are 'dos and don'ts' and both are necessary—indeed, we must avoid the idea that only the nurture of what is good is important. Gardeners will understand the idea of the necessity of removing weeds as well as pruning the roses (see Jesus' words in John 15:1–2).

Paul also stresses the need to avoid any gap between the 'private' and 'public' life of a person. He describes appetites and attitudes (v. 7), the managing of which are a matter of Christian discipleship, as well as more public and visible responsibilities (v. 9). What is important here is the consistency between belief and behaviour so that, whether in leadership or in everyday life, Christians are known to be authentic or, to put it more informally, the real thing.

Prayer

Lord, you have called us to follow you and to let your Spirit touch every part of our lives. Give leaders integrity and wisdom so that they make choices in the light of your holiness and grace, for Jesus Christ's sake. Amen

Andrew John

TITUS 1:10–15 (TNIV, ABRIDGED)

Healthy choices

For there are many rebellious people, full of meaningless talk and deception, especially those of the circumcision group. They must be silenced, because they are disrupting whole households by teaching things they ought not to teach—and that for the sake of dishonest gain. One of Crete's own prophets has said it: 'Cretans are always liars, evil brutes, lazy gluttons.' He has surely told the truth! Therefore rebuke them sharply, so that they will be sound in the faith... To the pure, all things are pure, but to those who are corrupted and do not believe, nothing is pure. In fact, both their minds and consciences are corrupted.

Reflecting on the consequences of a life uncontrolled by Christ leads Paul to the sharpest words he has in this letter. He has a particular group in mind—namely, those in the 'circumcision group' (v. 10) who appear more interested in 'Jewish myths' (v. 14) than the truth. They seem to be motivated by self interest (v. 11) and are committed to wrong beliefs (v. 10), but are also consumed and polluted by their own actions (v. 16).

Paul's language again draws a connection between the state of a person's life and the inevitable consequences in terms of ministry. In what way is this true? The question takes us to our key verse, verse 15, in which Paul explains that a corrupted life is disabling, as such people are unable to know the difference between good and bad, true and false, goodness and corruption. Paul's intention in this passage is not to induce inappropriate feelings of guilt, but, rather, provide a solution to a problem. Leaders must be people who make healthy choices embedded in their hearts and minds. There are few greater encouragements to younger Christians than seeing leaders who lead by example. They show a way of following Christ that is not naive, but attractive and challenging, which equips us for better service.

Prayer

Save us, Lord, from getting caught up in squabbles and disputes that bring you and us no credit. Give us a heart that is content only when walking close to you in humility and truth. Amen

ANDREW JOHN

TITUS 2:1–5 (TNIV)

Winning with words and actions

You, however, must teach what is appropriate to sound doctrine. Teach the older men to be temperate, worthy of respect, self-controlled, and sound in faith, in love and in endurance. Likewise, teach the older women to be reverent in the way they live, not to be slanderers or addicted to much wine, but to teach what is good. Then they can urge the younger women to love their husbands and children, to be self-controlled and pure, to be busy at home, to be kind, and to be subject to their husbands, so that no one will malign the word of God.

I remember the great but controversial American cyclist Lance Armstrong being interviewed. He described the punishing regime necessary to become the best and the difference between him and other cyclists—motivation. As I recall, he wondered if his competitors were, like him, sticking to the training schedule, even on Christmas day.

In this passage, both motivation and behaviour are important. It is easy to understand because it seems rooted in a time in which human relationships were conducted in ways that were very different from how we do so today. For example, we would want to say much more about the wrongness of slavery than this chapter goes on to do (vv. 9–10). It might also seem inappropriate to place men and women in social boxes in a seemingly unhelpfully constraining way. How, then, should we honour this teaching?

Let me suggest two ways. First, Paul is passionate that the word of God should not be reviled (v. 5), nor should God's people provide room for scandal (v. 8). This principle has enduring value because it describes our responsibility to be above reproach. Put more simply, do our actions dishonour Christ? Then, positively, Paul argues that our conduct should actually commend the Lord—he uses the word 'attractive' (v. 10) to highlight the positive impact we may have. It is an extraordinary thought, that we have such power to both dishonour and commend the Saviour.

Prayer

Lord Jesus, deepen my love for you and may it translate into service that brings you honour and praise. Make this my motivation and aim. Amen

ANDREW JOHN

Titus 2:11–15 (TNIV)

The end is in sight

For the grace of God has appeared that offers salvation to all people. It teaches us to say 'No' to ungodliness and worldly passions, and to live self-controlled, upright and godly lives in this present age, while we wait for the blessed hope—the appearing of the glory of our great God and Saviour, Jesus Christ, who gave himself for us to redeem us from all wickedness and to purify for himself a people that are his very own, eager to do what is good. These, then, are the things you should teach. Encourage and rebuke with all authority. Do not let anyone despise you.

In this great passage, Paul holds two key beliefs together as a foundation for what he has been commending to Titus. He also provides a framework within which Christian obedience occurs. The two beliefs are the appearances of Jesus—his first coming for all people ('the grace of God', v. 11) and his second coming as glorious victor (v. 13). We should note how Paul attaches Christ's initial appearance to what he has been previously saying. By his grace we can say 'yes' to God and 'no' to unrighteousness. The end in sight is his second coming—the blessed hope that gives us purpose and motivation now.

The familiar saying 'show me, don't tell me' encourages us to cut through words to action, and Paul's point is similar but better still. The grace of God does much more than simply inform or direct us; it enables us. Thus, we can draw on the strength of this grace to sustain us as we hope for the second appearance of Jesus who, in the words of the apostles' creed, 'will judge the living and the dead'. Our journey of faith and our being fashioned into his likeness will continue until he returns.

So, this is our challenge: to grasp how Christ gives us the means to follow him and make faithful choices that must be seen in the light of eternity.

Prayer

Living God, strengthen my faith and help me see the connection between these great truths and my everyday choices. When that vision fades, stand ever closer to me, I pray. Amen

Andrew John

TITUS 3:1–2 (TNIV)

Engaging to win

Remind the people to be subject to rulers and authorities, to be obedient, to be ready to do whatever is good, to slander no one, to be peaceable and considerate, and always to be gentle towards everyone.

Here, Paul addresses how Christians should behave in public life. As we have already considered, this is a consequence of Christian faith and designed to commend the Lord Jesus Christ, so that his followers might be above reproach.

We must be careful to neither dismiss Paul's injunctions here as overly simple, nor imagine that there is nothing further to say on this issue. Paul's counsel has two elements. First, ensuring that Christians do not behave inappropriately (v. 2, for example, we must slander no one) and, second—and more positively—we should be committed to good works (v. 1, 'be ready to do whatever is good').

What motivates these commands is the obedience of faith (Romans 1:5). Of course, this way of thinking is not absolute and, historically, Christians faced with unjust governments have been prepared to disobey civil authorities. The most notable example, perhaps, is that of Dietrich Bonhoeffer, who was persuaded that nothing less than active and violent opposition to the Nazis was the most Christian response. His decision cost him his life and is a stark reminder that obedience to Christ can be supremely costly.

Jesus employed the imagery of salt and light to show how disciples could transform situations and structures: 'You are the salt of the earth… You are the light of the world… let your light shine before others, that they may… glorify your Father in heaven' (Matthew 5:13–16). There can be little doubt that the scriptures emphasise we should be fully engaged with the world in order to win and transform it. All too often, we tend to assume that faith prevents us from 'getting our hands dirty', whereas the opposite is actually true.

Prayer

Lord Jesus, give me wisdom to discern how best to honour you in my life. Help me to see the connections between my faith in you and my attitudes to the world. Amen

ANDREW JOHN

Friday 7 September

TITUS 3:3–7 (TNIV)

A gospel to change us

At one time we too were foolish, disobedient, deceived and enslaved by all kinds of passions and pleasures. We lived in malice and envy, being hated and hating one another. But when the kindness and love of God our Saviour appeared, he saved us, not because of righteous things we had done, but because of his mercy. He saved us through the washing of rebirth and renewal by the Holy Spirit, whom he poured out on us generously through Jesus Christ our Saviour, so that, having been justified by his grace, we might become heirs having the hope of eternal life.

I have visited clergy whose studies might be thought good examples of creative chaos. They appear to know where things are—just about! Paul's development of his previous point brings the far less creative side of chaos into view. In fact, it is a chaos that is paralysing and destructive, but aptly describes our life before we met Christ. His message pulls no punches: a Christless life can result in terrible attitudes within us and to us being subjected to them by others. Paul, however, contrasts this with his key point, which is that Christ has changed us. This change has two elements. First, is the justifying work of Jesus, whose death brings forgiveness and hope (v. 7). Second (but strongly connected to the first point), is the work of the Holy Spirit, renewing and cleansing (v. 5).

This is a wonderful statement of the gospel, which brings us the hope of eternal life, but we should notice that the contrast means this personal transformation affects all of life. It is the gospel that allows us to cease being morally confused and chaotic and, instead, be restored to the life that God had planned for us. We can see, therefore, that there is no room for 'private faith' and—as we reflected yesterday—full engagement with the world is a direct consequence of belonging to Christ.

Prayer

Heavenly Father, thank you for the gift of your Son and your Spirit, whose work in us completely transforms our lives. Give us grace to continue in this faith and to be people of transformation. Amen

ANDREW JOHN

Saturday 8 September

Titus 3:8–11 (TNIV)

Peddlers of minutiae

This is a trustworthy saying. And I want you to stress these things, so that those who have trusted in God may be careful to devote themselves to doing what is good. These things are excellent and profitable for everyone. But avoid foolish controversies and genealogies and arguments and quarrels about the law, because these are unprofitable and useless. Warn divisive people once, and then warn them a second time. After that, have nothing to do with them. You may be sure that such people are warped and sinful; they are self-condemned.

One of the extraordinary characteristics of Christians and churches is our willingness to argue the minutest point possible. And very often we are all too ready to fall out or, worse, be divided on the matter. Paul's words of constraint here are highly relevant to us today and show the futility of such thinking. At the same time, he provides a kind of response to counter the tendency he describes and so his words assume a positive note, even if they appear bracingly direct.

The context of this passage is arguing over genealogies and points of law, but the principle surely has much wider application. Whenever we concentrate on minor points, we spend time on things that are unfruitful. There is also a danger that matters of first importance—the gospel and pillars of faith—become lost or hidden. So, Paul provides a response to this. In the first instance, it is one of confrontation, but, eventually, he decides to leave the peddlers of minutiae well alone. Such an approach might not sit easily with us, but there is real wisdom here because Paul's concern is for unity and also focus. In other words, he wants the core elements of the faith to stand centre stage and nothing must get in the way of that. We should, however, also focus all our energies on fruitful discussions and endeavour. How much time could churches release for mission if we acted like this? It is a sobering thought, is it not?

Prayer

Lord God, help me to be clear on the essentials, generous regarding secondary matters and, above all, not confuse the two. Forgive my own shortcomings, in Jesus' name. Amen

Andrew John

Titus 3:12–15 (TNIV)

Daily bread

As soon as I send Artemas or Tychicus to you, do your best to come to me at Nicopolis, because I have decided to winter there. Do everything you can to help Zenas the lawyer and Apollos on their way and see that they have everything they need. Our people must learn to devote themselves to doing what is good, in order to provide for urgent needs and not live unproductive lives. Everyone with me sends you greetings. Greet those who love us in the faith. Grace be with you all.

Paul concludes with a number of typically personal remarks and some final instructions for his younger colleague. Although they do not carry the seriousness of his earlier comments or the weight of his deeper reading of God's plan for salvation, these personal remarks are nonetheless important. They show that Paul is no 'go it alone Christian', but has others with whom he shares the ministry. There is no doubt that when leaders become isolated, they are the weaker for it. Elsewhere, Paul powerfully conveys a picture of the Church as a body in which the parts are interdependent (1 Corinthians 12:14–21) and this includes leaders, who need others to support them and from whom they can draw encouragement and wisdom.

Here we also see how Paul, to the last, has grounded his faith in practical ways (v. 14). The daily details may not seem the most exciting aspect of ministry, but they are essential. Elsewhere, Paul makes the same point (Galatians 2:10), so this is no one-off instruction but, rather, a clear reflection of Christ-like service. When churches are captivated by the depths of gospel grace and make 'the daily necessities' part of how they express their faith, there is something deeply attractive about it. This kind of Christian faith pleases God and is often a greater witness than words alone. It is the kind of living to which we are all called. So, today, how are you going to respond to this call afresh?

Prayer

Generous God, as you have given me so much, give me a will to respond in like manner so that I may do your will and others might be blessed. For Christ's sake. Amen

Andrew John

Our Creator God

Many of us watch popular science programmes on television and we are constantly impressed by the wonders of the universe disclosed by modern science. Scripture also has a great deal to say about the universe as God's creation and about God the Creator. I find that the story told by science and that told by theology complement each other quite beautifully.

The universe was awesome to the biblical writers and it ought to be just as awesome, if not more so, to us who know so much more about it. Scripture, however, is primarily concerned with the place of humans in the cosmos. Given the vastness and mystery of the universe, humans are uniquely privileged as we are made in God's image. Through our sin, however, we not only wreak havoc with our own lives and tarnish that image but also our relationship with non-human creation is damaged. We find ourselves 'dislocated' from creation and have to wrestle with the problem of suffering. Moreover, we need more urgently than ever to take seriously our God-given responsibilities towards creation.

Despite our sin, God loves us and cares intimately for each one of us. Throughout the Old Testament, he was working through his people, Israel. The redemption of the world is foreshadowed by the mighty acts of God to bring his people out of slavery and exile.

The most amazing claim of the Christian faith is that, in order to put things right, God becomes incarnate in the person of Jesus Christ, lives a perfect human life, dies an agonising death on the cross and rises again as the 'first fruits' of the new creation. Jesus is both the Word and the Wisdom of God and, among many 'types' of Christ in the Old Testament, perhaps Job, the archetypal innocent sufferer, stands out.

Creation is the work of the triune God. The second person of the Trinity, the Word, who upholds the universe in existence, became human to redeem us and bring all of creation to its ultimate destiny. The Spirit who swept over the face of the waters at the beginning changes us from the inside. Glory to the Father and to the Son and to the Holy Spirit! Amen

Rodney Holder

GENESIS 1:1–5 (NRSV)

God saw that it was good

In the beginning when God created the heavens and the earth, the earth was a formless void and darkness covered the face of the deep, while a wind from God swept over the face of the waters. Then God said, 'Let there be light'; and there was light. And God saw that the light was good; and God separated the light from the darkness. God called the light Day, and the darkness he called Night.

The Bible opens with this majestic sweep of creation. It is a literary masterpiece, describing creation from a theological perspective, so it is a mistake to read it as if it were some quasi-scientific text, telling us literally how the world was made.

Genesis 1 needs to be placed in the context in which it was written, which was probably during the Babylonian exile. In the Babylonian myth, Marduk, the chief god, defeated the sea goddess, Tiamat, in battle, sliced her in two and created the earth and sky from the two halves. Later he answered the gods' complaints about their heavy workload by creating humans from the blood of another dead god to do it for them.

The Genesis narrative could not be more different. First, there is only one God, not many warring gods. Second, God repeatedly sees that what he has made is good. In contrast, creation for the Babylonians is evil because it was created from the evil goddess's entrails. Third, in Genesis, humans are made in the image of God and given supreme authority to rule over the rest of creation as God's viceregents (v. 26).

Early church theologians, such as Augustine, realised that this passage could not be read literally. For example, on Day 1 God creates day and night, but the sun only appears on Day 4. The sun and moon are not even named but are called 'lights' because, in Babylonian cosmology, they were gods to be worshipped.

It is truly awe-inspiring that the majestic God, who is beyond space and time, *spoke* creation into being and gave humans such exalted status and responsibility over the rest of his wonderful creation.

Reflection

'O Lord, how manifold are your works! In wisdom you have made them all' (Psalm 104:24).

RODNEY HOLDER

GENESIS 2:7 (NRSV)

Humans are unique

Then the Lord God formed man from the dust of the ground, and breathed into his nostrils the breath of life; and the man became a living being.

If anything should convince us that the early chapters of Genesis should not be taken literally, it is the fact that after the sublime creation story of Genesis 1 comes a completely different story in Genesis 2. As before, the important question is, 'What does this teach us theologically?'

First, we should note the contrast between the transcendence of God in Genesis 1 and his immanence in Genesis 2—3. God comes close to humans in the second account, being given a personal name, Yahweh, and 'walking in the garden at the time of the evening breeze' (3:8).

Second, as Dietrich Bonhoeffer noted, scripture is even more materialistic about the human person than Darwin! Christians sometimes think having an animal ancestry is demeaning to humans, but Genesis traces our origin to the dust on the ground! The material world is good in Christian theology, unlike in ancient paganism or Platonism, and that was supremely demonstrated when 'the Word became flesh' (John 1:14). We should not reject our bodies but celebrate our bodily existence.

Third, humans are unique in possessing God's breath of life. The man is to till and keep the garden (2:15) and he names the animals that God creates, so demonstrating his oversight of God's world in a different way from Genesis 1. Ultimately, it is woman who is the suitable companion for the man (2:23–24). Jesus upholds the sanctity of marriage—God's wonderful gift to humans in creation (Matthew 19:3–9)—by appealing to this passage.

In Genesis 3, the relationship God intended is broken by human sin. To me, Adam (Hebrew for 'man') in this story is best interpreted as Everyman. As Bonhoeffer says, 'We ourselves are the ones who are affected, are intended, are addressed, accused, condemned, expelled' (*Creation and Fall*, 1997). Every one of us rebels against God. Ultimately, this fundamental human predicament is addressed when God comes in Christ to live the perfect human life and redeem us.

Prayer

Lord, thank you that you love me, sinner that I am.

RODNEY HOLDER

Wednesday 12 September

PSALM 8:3–5 (NRSV)

It is awesome

When I look at your heavens, the work of your fingers, the moon and the stars that you have established; what are human beings that you are mindful of them, mortals that you care for them? Yet you have made them a little lower than God, and crowned them with glory and honour.

It is sometimes said that, as science discovers more and more about how the universe works, God gets pushed into ever narrower corners since there is so much less for him to do. That is nonsense, since God is the author of everything there is, including the laws of science. It is like claiming that Shakespeare had nothing to do with *Hamlet* because we do not see him busily doing things during the performance. Alternatively, to use the example of scientist and theologian John Polkinghorne, understanding how burning gas heats the water in a kettle does not explain why the kettle is boiling—it is because I want a cup of tea! A scientific explanation in no way competes with an explanation in terms of personal agency.

The author of Psalm 8 was struck with awe and wonder at the night sky. I would be surprised if we did not share the same feeling, even if it is harder for many of us to escape the light pollution of our cities and really see the heavens in all their glory. Also, our awe and wonder is enhanced, not diminished, by our scientific knowledge.

For example, we know that our own sun, which is a very ordinary star, is a giant ball of energy some 860,000 miles across. In its core, the sun converts 600 million tons of hydrogen into helium every second by nuclear fusion, resulting in a power output of about 400 million million million million watts. Furthermore, there are 10,000 million million million stars in the observable universe!

The remarkable thing is that this awesome Creator God cares at all for human beings, let alone 'crowns them with glory and honour'. Yet he does care, down to the smallest detail. As Jesus tells us, even the hairs of our head are counted (Matthew 10:30).

Reflection

Despite the vastness of the universe, God cares for every detail of my life.

RODNEY HOLDER

PSALM 19:1–4 (NRSV)

Creation reveals God

The heavens are telling the glory of God; and the firmament proclaims his handiwork. Day to day pours forth speech, and night to night declares knowledge. There is no speech, nor are there words; their voice is not heard; yet their voice goes out through all the earth, and their words to the end of the world.

The heavens, in all their splendour, testify to their majestic creator. The 16th-century theologian John Calvin said that human beings possess a God-given '*sensus divinitatis*'—an awareness of God. It is by means of this awareness that we can perceive this wonderful universe is God's creation. Calvin also said that the creation is the 'theatre of God's glory'. Today's passage tells us that creation reveals its creator wordlessly. Paul says that 'faith comes from what is heard, and what is heard comes through the word of Christ', but then, quite remarkably, cites this passage from Psalm 19 to say that people have heard of Christ through the creation (Romans 10:17–18)!

A remarkable insight from modern cosmology is that the universe needs to be the size it is—with its 100,000 million galaxies—and the age it is (some 13.7 billion years) in order for us to exist. Yet creation does not exist solely for us; it exists to glorify God and God glories in his own handiwork. Thus, in Job 38:26–27, we read that God brings 'rain… on the desert, which is empty of human life, to satisfy the waste and desolate land, and to make the ground put forth grass'. God provides food and wine for humans (Psalm 104:14–15), but he also feeds the lions (v. 21; Job 38:39–40).

Psalm 19 switches effortlessly from the heavens to the moral law: 'The law of the Lord is perfect, reviving the soul' (v. 7) and keeping God's law brings joy and reward. Immanuel Kant wrote, 'Two things fill the mind with ever new and increasing wonder and awe, the more often and the more seriously reflection concentrates upon them: the starry heaven above me and the moral law within me' (*Critique of Practical Reason*, 1788).

Reflection

Let us seek to obey God's moral commandments, just as the heavenly bodies obey the laws God has decreed for them.

RODNEY HOLDER

ISAIAH 40:12, 26 (NRSV)

God's supreme power

> Who has measured the waters in the hollow of his hand and marked off the heavens with a span, enclosed the dust of the earth in a measure, and weighed the mountains in scales and the hills in a balance?... Lift up your eyes on high and see: Who created these? He who brings out their host and numbers them, calling them all by name; because he is great in strength, mighty in power, not one is missing.

Frequently in scripture, God confronts humans with the vastness and magnificence of the created order, and today's passage is an example. The context is the Hebrews' exile in Babylon. Their situation is terrible in the extreme. Their temple has been destroyed, their monarchy abolished, and they are now captives in a foreign land. How can all this possibly square with their knowledge of God and his promises to them?

The message about creation is not just there for its own sake. It is a message of encouragement because the prophet reminds them that their God is 'the everlasting God, the Creator of the ends of the earth' (v. 28). God's supreme power in creation tells us that he is also supremely powerful to save. To this God, the nations that oppress his people are 'like a drop from a bucket, and are accounted as dust on the scales' (v. 15). They are 'less than nothing' (v. 17). How can it be a problem for this God to rescue his people from tyranny?

The development of the universe from the Big Bang to the evolution of humans, the domain of the natural sciences, is the story of God bringing new things into being through the unfolding processes of nature. God has endowed nature with immense potentiality and creativity. That creativity in nature is mirrored in God's doing something new in history (42:9). He uses the pagan King Cyrus, called God's 'anointed' (or 'Messiah'), to bring about his people's homecoming and restoration.

We, too, can have confidence in the same all-powerful God to bring us through our tribulations and restore us.

Reflection

God is beyond space and time; God is beyond matter and words, yet he cares for me every moment of every day.

RODNEY HOLDER

JOHN 1:1–3, 14 (NRSV)

The Creator came to earth

> In the beginning was the Word, and the Word was with God, and the Word was God. He was in the beginning with God. All things came into being through him, and without him not one thing came into being... And the Word became flesh and lived among us, and we have seen his glory, the glory as of a father's only son, full of grace and truth.

This astonishing passage is the New Testament mirror of the creation story of Genesis 1. It tells us something at once utterly profound and utterly mind-blowing: it identifies the *Logos* or Word, which Greek readers of the Gospel would have understood as the rational principle of order behind the universe, with a human person—Jesus Christ. The one through whom this whole vast cosmos—from the tiniest subatomic particle to the furthest galaxy 13 billion light years away—came into existence has walked the earth as a human being.

Some cosmologists say that the universe is eternal or it is one of many universes (comprising a 'multiverse'), eternally coming and going out of existence. For us, however, Jesus Christ alone is eternal and being apart from his will, nothing else would exist at all.

The God in whom Christians believe is not some great experimenter in the sky—a cosmic puppeteer remote from his creation and impervious to his creatures' sufferings. No; while remaining fully God, he has also become fully human. He has lived a human life, suffered rejection by his own people (v. 11), wept over the death of a friend (11:35) and been brutally scourged and crucified.

'We have seen his glory,' John says, and, as his Gospel unfolds, it becomes plain that Jesus' glory is revealed most fully on the cross. It is when Jesus is lifted up on the cross that he draws all people to himself (12:32). From the cross, he recreates humanity, winning our forgiveness, sending his Spirit to change us from the inside and transforming our destiny beyond the grave. What an amazing Creator God!

Prayer

Father, thank you for the wonder of creation and the wonder of recreation and forgiveness in Christ.

RODNEY HOLDER

HEBREWS 1:1–4 (NRSV, ABRIDGED)

Creator, sustainer and redeemer

Long ago God spoke to our ancestors… by the prophets, but in these last days he has spoken to us by a Son, whom he appointed heir of all things, through whom he also created the worlds. He is the reflection of God's glory and the exact imprint of God's very being, and he sustains all things by his powerful word. When he had made purification for sins, he sat down at the right hand of the Majesty on high, having become as much superior to angels as the name he has inherited is more excellent than theirs.

Jesus is the radiance, the shining out of God's glory, showing us what God is like because he himself is God. He is the perfect icon, the exact representation of God's being and, when we look at Christ, we see the Father. The Son is also eternal; he was present in the beginning. Indeed, as we saw from John's Gospel yesterday, he is the living Word, the *Logos* through whom all things were made. Now we read that this powerful Word sustains the universe, keeping it going and holding all existence in being day by day. It is that same creative power of God that gave Christ the authority to overcome our sin. By his death and resurrection to new life, Jesus has brought about our forgiveness and salvation.

Nothing we have done or will do is too much for the Creator and Saviour of the world to deal with. What a liberating truth! We are free to live our lives to glorify our wonderful Lord, who is seated in majesty, but closer than any human companion. Yet, the world is a tough place; life is uncertain. Many of us have worries about finances, anxiety about health, concerns for the political instability, fighting and terrorism in so many parts of the world. We need not feel insecure or helpless, however, because Jesus has been through the darkest experiences, he understands and he is with us in our dark places to help us through them. He is the powerful creator and he will bring us peace and joy now and into eternity.

Prayer

Lord, may I focus not on problems but on your liberating power.

RODNEY HOLDER

Monday 17 September

PROVERBS 8:1, 23, 27–31 (NRSV, ABRIDGED)

God's wisdom

Does not wisdom call?… I was set up, at the first, before the beginning of the earth… When [God] established the heavens, I was there… when he made firm the skies above, when he established the fountains of the deep when he marked out the foundations of the earth, then I was beside him, like a master worker; and I was daily his delight, rejoicing before him always, rejoicing in his inhabited world and delighting in the human race.

Hebrews 1:2 tells that the universe was made through Christ, and his being the mediator of creation links him to the personification of Wisdom in the Old Testament. In our passage, Wisdom is a voice calling from before our universe existed. It is hard to imagine the age of the earth, let alone anything pre-existing it, so here we touch on a great mystery. We begin to sense the wonder and deep holiness of our God. How amazing to think of a time before time, before the sight of a star-spangled sky, before the rush of mighty winds, before the majestic surgings of oceans, before the vast height of mountains.

Before the beginning, there was nothing material, but there was God—God existing eternally in the communion of love within his own being, delighting in Wisdom, in the master builder about to exercise incredible creative power. As the creation emerged, God rejoiced in the inhabited world and delighted in human beings, whom he had created in his own likeness to live in love and fellowship with him.

God also delights in you. Many of us think that we fail too often to be worthy of God, but the truth is he is delighted with us. Yes, we are often unworthy of being in God's presence, but the same power that brought all that is into being is available to help us change. Just as a parent, delighting in a toddler's first steps, picking them up when they fall, so God will rescue us each time we fall and set us off afresh to live for him.

Prayer

O Lord, the glorious Creator, help me to live a life worthy of your love and delight, today and always. Amen

RODNEY HOLDER

JOB 38:1–2, 4, 31, 33 (NRSV, ABRIDGED)

Beyond understanding

> Then the Lord answered Job... 'Who is this that darkens counsel by words without knowledge?... Where were you when I laid the foundation of the earth? Tell me, if you have understanding... Can you bind the chains of the Pleiades, or loose the cords of Orion?... Do you know the ordinances of the heavens? Can you establish their rule on the earth?'

The most perplexing problem for faith is that of suffering. In Job, we meet the innocent sufferer and learn that it is all right to complain to God about our suffering. The pious theoretical answers—such as that Job must have sinned and brought it on himself—were offered by his so-called comforters, but, in the end, Job is vindicated and his friends are condemned. The book does not offer its own alternative theoretical answer. Instead, God confronts Job with his overwhelming power and wisdom and the mystery of creation. How can we hope to understand this God, who created this vast universe and is so lofty and majestic?

The astonishing discoveries of modern science give us an insight into the wisdom of God undreamed of by our ancestors, yet the answer to one question invariably leads to ten more! As Isaac Newton famously said, 'I seem to have been only like a boy playing on the seashore, and diverting myself in now and then finding a smoother pebble or a prettier shell than ordinary, whilst the great ocean of truth lay all undiscovered before me.'

The questions God poses to Job are heavily ironical: 'Where is the way to the dwelling of light...? Surely you know, for you were born then, and the number of your days is great!' (vv. 19, 21). Compared with God's wisdom and power, human knowledge and power are utterly insignificant. Ultimately, resolution for Job comes with God's self-revelation to him. Job says: 'I had heard of you by the hearing of the ear, but now my eyes see you; therefore I despise myself and repent in dust and ashes' (42:5–6). So it is for us, who wrestle now with our sufferings, but 'then we will see face to face' (1 Corinthians 13:12).

Prayer

Lord, help me to trust to your wisdom in all circumstances.

RODNEY HOLDER

COLOSSIANS 1:15–17, 19–20 (NRSV, ABRIDGED)

The Creator crucified

He is the image of the invisible God, the firstborn of all creation; for in him all things in heaven and on earth were created, things visiblc and invisible, whether thrones or dominions or rulers or powers—all things have been created through him and for him. He himself is before all things, and in him all things hold together... For in him all the fullness of God was pleased to dwell, and through him God was pleased to reconcile to himself all things... making peace through the blood of his cross.

This passage—probably an early church creed—is another of the New Testament's great expressions of what theologians call a 'high Christology'. Indeed, the status of Jesus Christ—the image (Greek 'icon') of the invisible God—could not be more exalted. Originally, God created human beings in his own image, but that image is tarnished because of human sin. Jesus Christ, God's own Son, is the perfect image of God.

The universe was created through Christ and for Christ and 'holds together' in him moment by moment. Sometimes atheist scientists say they have eliminated God if they have eliminated a first moment at the Big Bang, perhaps through some theory that removes it. But that is to misunderstand the Christian doctrine of creation, which says that every moment exists only by the will of God. The universe would collapse into nothingness unless it were upheld by Christ. God is continuously active in the world, not just 'lighting the blue touchpaper' at the Big Bang.

Chief among God's actions is 'reconciling all things to himself'. Yesterday we noted that Job was the innocent sufferer. Jesus is the innocent sufferer who 'makes peace by the blood of his cross'. As G.K. Chesterton notes, 'In the book of Job is foreshadowed that better doctrine full of a dark chivalry that he that bore the worst that men can suffer was the best that bore the form of man' (*Leviathan and the Hook*, 1905). Our salvation was procured by Jesus' suffering and is made effectual in our lives through the action of the Holy Spirit.

Reflection

Only the suffering God can help.

Dietrich Bonhoeffer, *Letters and Papers from Prison* (1971 edn)

RODNEY HOLDER

JOEL 1:11, 18; 2:12–13 (NRSV)

Caring for creation

Be dismayed, you farmers, wail, you vine-dressers, over the wheat and the barley; for the crops of the field are ruined... How the animals groan! The herds of cattle wander about because there is no pasture for them... Yet even now, says the Lord, return to me with all your heart, with fasting, with weeping, and with mourning; rend your hearts and not your clothing. Return to the Lord, your God, for he is gracious and merciful, slow to anger, and abounding in steadfast love, and relents from punishing.

I write at a time when once more famine is ravaging East Africa. Our hearts go out to the starving children we see on our TV screens and, I trust, we are as generous as we can be in our response to the appeals we hear for aid. The crisis may have passed when you read this, but such crises repeat all too often.

God's creation is good and the world is provided with abundant resources so that there should be enough for everyone. God has also given us the ability to understand his world through the natural sciences, including agricultural science, and to use our knowledge for good.

We bring destruction on ourselves and our neighbours, however, by waging war and unfair economic practices—and it is usually the poor who suffer most. As a statement from Oxfam puts it: 'this crisis has been caused by people and policies, as much as by weather patterns'.

Scripture teaches that there is a dislocation between humans and the natural world because of human sin. It is remarkable that the passages speaking about this dislocation resonate today in a way never before experienced in history. Globally, we have overexploited and polluted the planet, creating dire consequences for future generations.

As our passage today indicates, we need to return to God, to honour him and follow his ways. Then, he says later in Joel, 'I will repay you for the years that the swarming locust has eaten... You shall eat in plenty and be satisfied, and praise the name of the Lord your God' (2:25–26).

Reflection

Do I take seriously my responsibility towards creation?

RODNEY HOLDER

Romans 8:18–21 (NRSV)

Liberation

I consider that the sufferings of this present time are not worth comparing with the glory about to be revealed to us. For the creation waits with eager longing for the revealing of the children of God; for the creation was subjected to futility, not of its own will but by the will of the one who subjected it, in hope that the creation itself will be set free from its bondage to decay and will obtain the freedom of the glory of the children of God.

The universe—God's wonderful creation—is not in the state that God ultimately intends for it. Yesterday we noted the dislocation between human beings and the creation seen in crop failure and famine.

Scientist-theologians such as John Polkinghorne argue that the creation comes as a 'package deal'. The natural world is a highly interlocked system in which such factors as death and disease provide the necessary conditions for novelty and growth. That is seen in the mass extinctions and suffering in the animal world, which seem to have been necessary precursors of the arrival of human beings on the planet through the evolutionary process. Nevertheless, we humans undoubtedly experience a much greater dislocation than we otherwise would because of human sin, and the 'subjection of creation to futility' may refer back to the consequences of the primordial sin described in Genesis 3:17–18.

It seems that creation cannot fulfil its ultimate destiny apart from human beings fulfilling theirs, which can only come about through the incarnation, death and resurrection of Christ. At the present time, the status of the 'children of God' is veiled. Christians are despised and persecuted by the world, but that will change. We suffer with Christ 'that we may also be glorified with him' (Romans 8:17). Our ultimate destiny is to share in God's glory and we have the foretaste and guarantee of that now through the indwelling Spirit (v. 26). One day, the children of God will be manifested to the whole creation, which will itself be transformed. Then, 'mourning and crying and pain will be no more' (Revelation 21:4).

Prayer

Thank you, Lord, for the promise of future glory.

Rodney Holder

REVELATION 21:1–4 (NRSV, ABRIDGED)

Our Recreator God

Then I saw a new heaven and a new earth; for the first heaven and the first earth had passed away, and the sea was no more. And I saw the holy city, the new Jerusalem, coming down out of heaven from God, prepared as a bride adorned for her husband. And I heard a loud voice from the throne saying, 'See, the home of God is among mortals... God himself will be with them; he will wipe every tear from their eyes. Death will be no more.'

Physicists tell us that, according to the second law of thermodynamics, as time passes, the universe is becoming more disordered. Ultimately, if left to its own devices, many billions of years from now, the universe will undergo a final 'heat death' in which nothing further of interest can happen.

Scripture assures us, however, that, at some point, God will do something radically new. There will be a new creation in which there will be no more death and decay—no more second law of thermodynamics! The one reason—but it is a mighty powerful reason—we can have confidence in this is that the future has already broken into the present and been witnessed, in the resurrection of Jesus.

Revelation 21 paints a beautiful picture of that new creation. Note that we are not promised a disembodied ghostly existence in some vague realm of spirits. The new creation is represented as a city, so it will be physical, just like the present. It will be made from the physical things from this creation, like the precious stones (vv. 18–21). Moreover, having physical bodies is part of what it means to be human. It is just that these bodies will be transformed so that they no longer suffer disease or wear out.

When scripture talks of the 'new' heaven and earth, as New Testament scholar John Sweet said, it does not mean the brand new, but the radically renewed. It is the glorious fulfilment and completion of what is already the case. As Paul says, 'if anyone is in Christ, there is a new creation' (2 Corinthians 5:17).

Reflection

Both we and the cosmos await our glorious consummation.

RODNEY HOLDER

2 Kings 5—8

The second book of Kings is the last of the group of books—Joshua, Judges, Samuel and Kings—sometimes known as the Former Prophets. It is a slightly misleading name as they are presented as historical accounts, though prophets do play a role, sometimes a very important role, in this history. They cover a very long period, from the settlement of Israel in Palestine after the exodus to the exile.

The books of Kings themselves cover around four centuries, from the death of David in the tenth century BC to the middle of the exile in Babylon in the sixth century BC. In terms of British history, it is like having one book covering the period from Henry VIII to World War II.

We should not forget that the historical books of the Bible are never history pure and simple (if there is any such thing!) The writers always have a theological point to make. In Kings, we can identify four main themes, which you might want to look out for as you read. The first is that the God of Israel is the only true God; and the second follows—true worship is offered to him alone, not any other gods. The third theme is that this is a moral universe. God lays down standards and punishes wrongdoers, but also has compassion. Finally, there is the theme of God's promise, made to the patriarchs and David.

The particular prophet of this part of the second book of Kings is Elisha. He is Elijah's 'apprentice', called to the prophetic ministry in 1 Kings 19:19–21. The stories of Elisha begin in 2 Kings 2 and continue into 2 Kings 13, which records his death. The stories in our part of 2 Kings are not necessarily in chronological order, so are best taken as a collection of separate stories, each one on its own terms.

Many of the stories are quite long, too, and you may well find it helpful to read the whole passage from which the readings come to get the wider picture. Elisha is doing God's work in a complex and sometimes dangerous world. With imagination, we can learn from his story for our own discipleship.

Helen Julian CSF

2 Kings 5:1–5 (NRSV)

High and mighty

> Naaman, commander of the army of the king of Aram, was a great man and in high favour with his master, because by him the Lord had given victory to Aram. The man, though a mighty warrior, suffered from leprosy. Now the Arameans on one of their raids had taken a young girl captive from the land of Israel, and she served Naaman's wife. She said to her mistress, 'If only my lord were with the prophet who is in Samaria! He would cure him of his leprosy.' So Naaman went in and told his lord just what the girl from the land of Israel had said. And the king of Aram said, 'Go then, and I will send along a letter to the king of Israel.'

Aram is what is now Syria, with its capital even then in Damascus. It is easy to miss the significance of the first sentence in the passage above. Aram and Israel were often at war with one another and here we are told that God has used Naaman, the Aramean commander, to defeat his own people. Perhaps this is a way of asserting the sovereignty of the Lord. Everything, whether success or defeat, is in his hands.

Naaman's 'leprosy' is unlikely to have been the disease we now call by that name as it would have made him an outcast from society, but he undoubtedly had a disfiguring and embarrassing skin disease. His power as a warrior, his favour with the king and his consequent high position could not exempt him from the disease and its consequences.

It is a good reminder of the basics of the human condition. Money, status and power can perhaps make some suffering easier to cope with, but they do not make anyone exempt from illness or sadness.

The servant girl's position is at the opposite end of the spectrum from Naaman—she has no name and is a servant in a foreign country. She has no power or influence, but knows the power of God and that he works through 'the prophet who is in Samaria' and is willing to help her master and captor.

Prayer

Sovereign God, help me to trust in your power
and not the power of the world.

Helen Julian CSF

2 Kings 5:5–7 (NRSV)

Power and paranoia

> [Naaman] went, taking with him ten talents of silver, six thousand shekels of gold, and ten sets of garments. He brought the letter to the king of Israel, which read, 'When this letter reaches you, know that I have sent to you my servant Naaman, that you may cure him of his leprosy.' When the king of Israel read the letter, he tore his clothes and said, 'Am I God, to give death or life, that this man sends word to me to cure a man of his leprosy? Just look and see how he is trying to pick a quarrel with me.'

Where does power really lie? The king of Aram, judging by his letter, seems to see the power of the prophet as a reflection of the power of the king of Israel. The prophet is, in his eyes, a servant of the king, to whom the power of healing really belongs. So it is not necessary even to mention the prophet, although the servant was clear that it was he who had the power to heal Naaman.

The presents that the king of Aram sends are huge, and they might in themselves have aroused the king of Israel's suspicions as to his real motives. A talent was the largest unit of weight in the near East, though its actual weight varied greatly, from 130 pounds in the old Babylonian system to 45 pounds in the latest Jewish system. So, Aram's gift could have been as much as 7 hundredweight of silver and 150 pounds of gold, though it may be that the storyteller exaggerated to increase the drama of the story.

The king of Israel (who was probably Jehoram) injects yet more drama. He allows his natural suspicion of a sometime enemy to take over and assumes the worst. He thinks that this can only be a ploy to justify further warfare as he will be unable to cure Naaman, which will give the king of Aram a reason to attack him and his country once more.

Those with power often assume that only those with equivalent power are any use to them and worth communicating with. This story shows how wrong that assumption is.

Reflection

What assumptions do you make about power?

Helen Julian CSF

2 Kings 5:8–11 (NRSV)

God's way of working

> But when Elisha the man of God heard that the king of Israel had torn his clothes, he sent a message to the king, 'Why have you torn your clothes? Let him come to me, that he may learn that there is a prophet in Israel.' So Naaman came with his horses and chariots, and halted at the entrance of Elisha's house. Elisha sent a messenger to him, saying, 'Go, wash in the Jordan seven times, and your flesh shall be restored and you shall be clean.' But Naaman became angry and went away, saying, 'I thought that for me he would surely come out, stand and call on the name of the Lord his God, and would wave his hand over the spot, and cure the leprosy!'

Elisha now steps out of the shadows. Until this point in the story he has not been named, though a reader of the whole book would know who was being referred to. His appearance is very self-assured. He sends a message to the king rather than go to the king himself and he asks Naaman to come to him. This is probably not what Naaman expected, but he arrives at the prophet's door. He comes not as a humble man in need of healing, but with his horses and chariots, in all his pomp. The fact that he can drive up to Elisha's door must mean that Elisha is either living in an isolated house or near the king's quarters. Anywhere else would have been too congested for chariots to pass through.

The unsettling of Naaman's sense of status continues. Elisha does not appear himself, but simply sends a messenger. This is the final straw; Naaman feels insulted. Expecting Elisha to come out 'for me' means literally for 'a person like me' and is very emphatic. He is protective of his status—how dare the prophet not come out and perform the proper ritual for healing!

Our sense of our position in the world and expectations of how God and God's 'agents' should deal with us can get in the way of what God is offering and how God wants to work in our lives.

Reflection

Do you find it unsettling, upsetting, that God appears to disregard hierarchy?

Helen Julian CSF

2 Kings 5:12–14 (NRSV)

Simple ways

[Naaman said] 'Are not Abana and Pharpar, the rivers of Damascus, better than all the waters of Israel? Could I not wash in them, and be clean?' He turned and went away in a rage. But his servants approached and said to him, 'Father, if the prophet had commanded you to do something difficult, would you not have done it? How much more, when all he said to you was, "Wash, and be clean"?' So he went down and immersed himself seven times in the Jordan, according to the word of the man of God; his flesh was restored like the flesh of a young boy, and he was clean.

Not only has Naaman himself been insulted, but so has his country and its rivers (Abana and Pharpar flow, respectively, north and south of Damascus). Things are not going well. At this crucial point, however, another servant steps in. The servant girl had compassion; this one has wisdom. He knows how to break through Naaman's indignation with a quiet word. Naaman pauses in his rage and thinks again. He goes to the Jordan as Elisha has instructed him, immerses himself seven times and the skin disease is cured. Not only is he no longer afflicted, but he is no longer ritually impure—he is both healed and clean.

The desire for the dramatic and the special can be a real block in our spiritual lives. Sometimes, of course, they do happen, but most of the time God and God's servants deal with us in very ordinary ways. We are asked to do normal mundane things for our well-being. We would often much prefer a dramatic instant cure—the healer calling on God's name, waving his or her hands over us—and whatever ails us, physical or spiritual, gone.

Far more often, we are the ones who must act. We listen, we hear, then we do our equivalent of going to the Jordan, undramatic as it is, immersing ourselves seven times.

We need to hear the servant's words just as Naaman did.

Reflection

Can you recall times when you demanded a dramatic intervention from God rather than cooperating with his simple way of healing or changing you?

Helen Julian CSF

2 Kings 5:15–19 (NRSV, abridged)

A realistic response

Then [Naaman] returned to the man of God... and said, 'Now I know that there is no God in all the earth except in Israel; please accept a present from your servant.' But he said, 'As the Lord lives, whom I serve, I will accept nothing!' He urged him to accept, but he refused. Then Naaman said, 'If not, please let two mule-loads of earth be given to your servant; for your servant will no longer offer burnt-offering or sacrifice to any god except the Lord. But may the Lord pardon your servant on one count: when my master goes into the house of Rimmon to worship there, leaning on my arm, and I bow down in the house of Rimmon may the Lord pardon your servant on this one count.' He said to him, 'Go in peace.'

Accepting a present from Naaman would imply that he had been healed by Elisha rather than God, so Elisha refuses.

He is also willing to be flexible, though. Naaman's request for two mule-loads of earth to take back to Aram reflects a belief that deities were linked to and only active in their particular land. Naaman asks for some of Israel's land, so that he can pray to Israel's God in a strange land. Elisha does not refuse this request or argue with him about his theology.

Then he goes even further. One of Naaman's tasks is to accompany the king to worship, the worship of Rimmon, which is probably a Jewish parody of Ramman, one of the titles of Hadad, the Syrian Baal. Normally the prophets are vehement in rejecting the worship of these pagan gods. Once again Elisha accepts Naaman's request, seeming to understand his situation, and gives his blessing to this compromise.

This book was written during the exile, so its writers stress that God is accessible everywhere. Perhaps in this story, though, there is also a recognition that sometimes in exile God's people are forced into compromising situations and God will understand if this is so.

Prayer

Lord of all times and all places, let me know you everywhere and in everything, even in what seems to deny you.

Helen Julian CSF

2 KINGS 6:1–7 (NRSV, ABRIDGED)

The God of small things

Now the company of prophets said to Elisha, 'As you see, the place where we live under your charge is too small for us. Let us go to the Jordan, and let us collect logs there... and build a place there for us to live.' He answered, 'Do so.'... When they came to the Jordan, they cut down trees. But as one was felling a log, his axehead fell into the water; he cried out, 'Alas, master! It was borrowed.' Then the man of God said, 'Where did it fall?' When he showed him the place, he cut off a stick, and threw it in there, and made the iron float. He said, 'Pick it up.' So he reached out his hand and took it.

Moving from Naaman's story, with its kings and high drama, to this one, is a bit of a jolt. It needs to be read as part of a different group of stories, centring on Elisha among the prophets, probably recounted verbally for generations before being written down. So, to look at this story with the same eyes as the previous one is to misunderstand it.

It could seem the kind of miracle that gives miracles a bad name. What is a lost axehead compared to the healing of illness or the intervention in matters of State, which we will move on to tomorrow?

The setting here is probably by the Jordan, around Jericho, where a group of prophets were attached to the shrine of Gilgal. Elisha gives his blessing to the project to build more shelters and goes with them to cut the timber. We can imagine the distress of the one whose axehead flies off into the water—not only has he lost a valuable tool but also it was not even his!

Elisha rescues both him and the axehead. As a man of God, he echoes God's concern for the details of others' lives—the need for shelter and help with the small disasters that befall them. The point of the story is not whether or not iron floats, but whether God cares or not. He does.

Reflection

How is God the God of small things in your life?

HELEN JULIAN CSF

Saturday 29 September

2 Kings 6:8–9, 11–13 (NRSV)

Who is the spy?

Once when the king of Aram was at war with Israel, he took counsel with his officers. He said, 'At such and such a place shall be my camp.' But the man of God sent word to the king of Israel, 'Take care not to pass this place, because the Arameans are going down there.'... The mind of the king of Aram was greatly perturbed because of this; he called his officers and said to them, 'Now tell me who among us sides with the king of Israel?' Then one of his officers said, 'No one, my lord king. It is Elisha, the prophet in Israel, who tells the king of Israel the words that you speak in your bedchamber.' He said, 'Go and find where he is; I will send and seize him.'

The uneasy peace of the Naaman story has broken down and the two countries are, once again, at war. It may be that this was less a full-scale war between two nations and more a series of border raids by nomads. Whatever the nature of the hostilities, Elisha is involved. His ministry has very wide scope, from recovering lost axeheads through to healing skin diseases and military intelligence.

This may not be quite our image of a prophet. We perhaps expect that they will confine themselves to 'religious' matters, but the well-being of God's people is God's concern, so Elisha is involved in protecting Israelite towns and villages against the marauding Arameans.

Once again, an anonymous 'servant'—one of the king's officers—seems to know more than the important leader. The king suspects treachery and is, understandably, very perturbed. This last word, which can also be translated 'troubled', is very strong. The king's mind is in a whirl, like a whirlwind.

Notice that the writer does not specify how Elisha knows the king's plans. It may be that his frequent travelling around the region and his many local contacts enabled him to organise an efficient intelligence service. God works through such 'natural' means as well as the supernatural means of dreams and visions.

Reflection

Are there areas of life in which you think Christians should not be involved?

Helen Julian CSF

2 KINGS 6:15–17 (NRSV)

The company of heaven

When an attendant of the man of God rose early in the morning and went out, an army with horses and chariots was all around the city. His servant said, 'Alas, master! What shall we do?' He replied, 'Do not be afraid, for there are more with us than there are with them.' Then Elisha prayed: 'O Lord, please open his eyes that he may see.' So the Lord opened the eyes of his servant, and he saw; the mountain was full of horses and chariots of fire all around Elisha.

The army with horses and chariots has been sent by the king of Aram to the city of Dothan, to capture Elisha. Then we have this famous, yet brief, story, told vividly and concisely.

We can imagine the attendant rising early, perhaps to prepare breakfast, and seeing the surrounding army. Terrified, he runs to find his master, who immediately reassures him—not just with words but also sight. The servant's eyes are opened and he sees that God's army is around Elisha, protecting him.

The story may remind us of the beginning of Elisha's ministry, when his master, Elijah, went up to heaven in a chariot of fire drawn by horses of fire (2 Kings 2:9–12). The fact that Elisha saw them then was a guarantee that he would inherit Elijah's spirit and his prophetic ministry. So the servant is being allowed to see what Elisha saw then and perhaps always or often sees—the normally invisible presence and work of God in his world.

'See' is a key word in this passage. The servant is not blind in any normal sense, yet Elisha prays God will open his eyes 'that he may see'. We talk about the 'real world', but which is the real world here? Is the reality the flesh and blood army of the Arameans or the protecting army of God? Faith sees the world differently and, for a brief period, the servant is privileged to see the world as Elisha sees it.

Prayer

God of hosts, as we worship today, may we know ourselves to be in the company of heaven, surrounded by your protection.

HELEN JULIAN CSF

2 KINGS 6:20–23 (NRSV, ABRIDGED)

Practical peacemaking

As soon as [the Arameans] entered Samaria, Elisha said, 'O Lord, open the eyes of these men so that they may see.' The Lord opened their eyes, and they saw that they were inside Samaria. When the king of Israel saw them he said to Elisha, 'Father, shall I kill them? Shall I kill them?' He answered, 'No! Did you capture with your sword and your bow those whom you want to kill? Set food and water before them so that they may eat and drink; and let them go to their master.' So he prepared for them a great feast... And the Arameans no longer came raiding into the land of Israel.

God can close eyes as well as open them. Between yesterday's passage and today's, Elisha has asked God to close the eyes of the attacking army, then led them to Samaria—a fortified city where the king of Israel is staying.

Then he prays that their temporary blindness may be lifted. The tables have been turned and they are now in the power of the Israelites. The king addresses Elisha with great deference, but his eager desire to kill them is not pleasing to the prophet. It is not right to kill even those whom you have captured yourself, let alone those who have been brought non-violently into your power.

The Arameans have failed in their task of capturing Elisha, so he can be generous. A banquet is prepared for them, then they are allowed to go home. As in the story of Naaman, representatives of the enemy are treated well. Having shared in a meal, they are less likely to come raiding again. The word translated 'Arameans' is, in fact, 'band of Arameans' and this, along with the word 'raiding', lends weight to the theory that these are raids by nomads rather than full-scale war between nations.

This is very practical peacemaking: no one is harmed on either side, and the enemy is treated with honour and respect, given not just food and water but also a great feast. Elisha the military strategist is also a peacemaker, with power over kings and armies.

Reflection

In what way are you a peacemaker?

HELEN JULIAN CSF

2 KINGS 6:24–27 (NRSV)

Dire straits

Some time later King Ben-hadad of Aram mustered his entire army; he marched against Samaria and laid siege to it. As the siege continued, famine in Samaria became so great that a donkey's head was sold for eighty shekels of silver, and one-fourth of a kab of dove's dung for five shekels of silver. Now as the king of Israel was walking on the city wall, a woman cried out to him, 'Help, my lord king!' He said, 'No! Let the Lord help you. How can I help you? From the threshing-floor or from the wine-press?'

If the previous conflict has been relatively small-scale and localised, this time it is definitely war. The entire Aramean army is involved and has been able to keep Samaria under siege for so long that all sources of food ('the threshing floor') have given out. The kings involved are Ben-Hadad II or III of Aram, and Jehoram, Jehoahaz or Joash of Israel.

Some of today's more adventurous chefs might rise to the challenge of making a meal of a donkey's head, but here it stands for something inedible that is still fetching a huge price, so bad are the shortages. At least it is clear what it is. The 'one-fourth of a kab of dove's dung' is much more puzzling. A kab is either two pints or two litres, so this is apparently half a pint to a pint of dove's droppings being sold for an ounce of silver. It may not be quite as strange as it sounds, though it is still a vivid sign of the depths of the people's need. 'Dove's dung' may be a popular name for carob pods or beans or for roasted chickpeas and there is a plant known in Arabic as dove's dung. So, it may at least have been edible, if appallingly expensive.

The king is accessible to his people, walking on the city wall, perhaps looking out in the hope that the siege might miraculously have been lifted. As he is powerless to bring that about, though, he is powerless to help his people. He can only suggest calling out to God.

Reflection

Do you only call on God when all else has failed?

HELEN JULIAN CSF

2 Kings 6:28–31 (NRSV)

Seeking a scapegoat

> But then the king asked [the woman], 'What is your complaint?' She answered, 'This woman said to me, "Give up your son; we will eat him today, and we will eat my son tomorrow." So we cooked my son and ate him. The next day I said to her, "Give up your son and we will eat him." But she has hidden her son.' When the king heard the words of the woman he tore his clothes—now since he was walking on the city wall, the people could see that he had sackcloth on his body underneath—and he said, 'So may God do to me, and more, if the head of Elisha son of Shaphat stays on his shoulders today.'

Now the full horror of war is graphically demonstrated. Cannibalism under the stress of famine or siege was not uncommon throughout the ancient world and not unknown in the Old Testament (Deuteronomy 28:53–57; Lamentations 4:10; Ezekiel 5:10). It is not surprising, however, that the stark horror of this brief story, told in such a matter of fact way by the woman, should so affect the king.

His sackcloth is a sign of penitence and his identification with the suffering people. The king has previously told the woman to call on God and now we can see that he has been following his own advice, praying in sackcloth for deliverance.

Then the story takes a strange turn. Why should the king, in his anguish, threaten Elisha? Earlier in this chapter he has addressed him with great respect as 'Father' and followed his instruction to let the Aramean raiders go home in safety. Perhaps he now regrets that generosity and blames Elisha for his advice? Perhaps he fears the people will turn on him and is trying to divert attention to a suitable scapegoat?

It is a not unusual human tendency to behave in this way. When things are going badly, some of us blame ourselves, while others lash out at those around them, looking for someone else to blame. The reality is often somewhere in the middle as rarely are we either entirely to blame or entirely innocent.

Prayer

God of judgment, help me to see clearly and acknowledge my part in the difficulties around me.

Helen Julian CSF

2 KINGS 8:7–11 (NRSV, ABRIDGED)

Burden of knowledge

Elisha went to Damascus while King Ben-hadad of Aram was ill. When it was told him, 'The man of God has come here,' the king said to Hazael, 'Take a present with you and go to meet the man of God. Inquire of the Lord through him, whether I shall recover from this illness.' So Hazael went to meet him, taking a present with him… forty camel loads. When he entered and stood before him, he said, 'Your son King Ben-hadad of Aram has sent me to you, saying, "Shall I recover from this illness?"' Elisha said to him, 'Go, say to him, "You shall certainly recover"; but the Lord has shown me that he shall certainly die.'… Then the man of God wept.

We do not have the space to include chapter 7 here, but it continues the siege story and is well worth reading for yourself. Elisha prophesies victory and is vindicated. This shows how he moves easily between the two kingdoms and is valued highly by those in power for his God-given gifts.

The dividing lines between faiths are fuzzy and fluid: here a pagan king sends a man to the Lord; in 2 Kings 1, Ahaziah sends someone to a foreign god. Both want to know if they will recover from illness.

The present—'forty camel loads'—is once again an exaggerated amount, probably meant to indicate great wealth and generosity. The story really turns on the double meaning of a Hebrew word in 8:8. The word *haya* can mean either 'live' or 'recover one's health'. Ben-hadad has in mind the former meaning; Elisha replies in terms of the latter meaning. This explains what seems a riddle in verse 10—that is, how can Elisha send a message to say that Ben-hadad will recover and also say that the Lord has shown him he will in fact die? His gifts of prophecy have put him in a very difficult position, as we will see in tomorrow's story. The king's illness is not to be fatal, but he is still about to die and Hazael, the messenger, is deeply implicated in his fate.

Reflection

Are there times when you have wished you did not know something? How did you deal with the unwelcome knowledge?

HELEN JULIAN CSF

2 KINGS 8:12–15 (NRSV, ABRIDGED)

Foreboding

Hazael asked, 'Why does my lord weep?' [Elisha] answered, 'Because I know the evil that you will do to the people of Israel; you will set their fortresses on fire, you will kill their young men with the sword, dash in pieces their little ones, and rip up their pregnant women.' Hazael said, 'What is your servant, who is a mere dog, that he should do this great thing?' Elisha answered, 'The Lord has shown me that you are to be king over Aram.' Then he left Elisha, and went to his master Ben-hadad... [and told him] 'He told me that you would certainly recover.' But the next day he took the bed-cover and dipped it in water and spread it over the king's face, until he died. And Hazael succeeded him.

Now we see the quandary in which Elisha found himself. He has knowledge of Hazael's future and it is a terrible picture. Hazael, who came out of nowhere, was not a member of the royal family, reigned for 40 years in Damascus and was a very great threat to Israel. The writer of Kings uses chilling language: 'In those days the Lord began to trim off parts of Israel. Hazael defeated them throughout the territory of Israel' (2 Kings 10:32). The perspective is the same as that at the beginning of our readings—there God used Naaman to punish his people for their sins; here he is using Hazael.

Hazael seems to be without scruples. He sees the terrible deeds that Elisha foretells him carrying out against Israel as 'this great thing'. I wonder how Elisha felt when he heard that Ben-hadad had died. Did he feel guilty that perhaps he had encouraged Hazael on his evil way?

In some sense this seems to have been preordained. Elijah had been told (1 Kings 19:15–16) that he would legitimate two coups, anointing Jehu as king over Israel and Hazael over Aram. It falls to his successor, Elisha, to see these things happen, though he does not in fact anoint Hazael. The prophet's role is often uncomfortable and sometimes dangerous.

Prayer

Lord of history, show me our times through your eyes.

HELEN JULIAN CSF

2 KINGS 8:16–19 (NRSV)

God's promise

In the fifth year of King Joram son of Ahab of Israel, Jehoram son of King Jehoshaphat of Judah began to reign. He was thirty-two years old when he became king, and he reigned for eight years in Jerusalem. He walked in the way of the kings of Israel, as the house of Ahab had done, for the daughter of Ahab was his wife. He did what was evil in the sight of the Lord. Yet the Lord would not destroy Judah, for the sake of his servant David, since he had promised to give a lamp to him and to his descendants for ever.

After some of the riveting stories of the previous chapters, these are perhaps the verses we are tempted to skip. They are full of unfamiliar names and we can soon become lost in the details of who was married to whom and who reigned when. Such summaries are common in the historical books, though, so presumably the writers felt that they had value. What can we learn from them?

Partly, of course, it is simply a matter of keeping the story straight. In this chapter of 2 Kings, we learn about the two Judean kings whose reigns overlapped with that of Jehoram of Israel, who has featured in some of our earlier stories. These summaries also alert us to the standing of the king: has he walked in the ways of God or in the ways of the gods of other nations?

This second reason is the only criterion for judgment in the eyes of the writer. It does not matter if the king was a great warrior or an excellent administrator or a skilful negotiator. The only thing that matters is whether he did evil or good in God's sight.

Here, however, there is a reminder of God's faithfulness, even in the face of Jehoram of Judah's faithlessness. Because of the promise to David made through Nathan, an earlier prophet—'I will establish the throne of his kingdom for ever' (2 Samuel 7:13)—God will not destroy Judah. The lamp (1 Kings 11:36) is a symbol of a representative of the house of David and God will ensure that it remains alight.

Reflection

How do we judge our rulers—by human standards or God's?

HELEN JULIAN CSF

The God of Isaac

When the people of Israel were in trouble in Egypt, trapped in wretched slavery, the writer of the book of Exodus tells us that God heard their groaning and 'remembered his covenant with Abraham, Isaac and Jacob' (Exodus 2:24). He called Moses to lead the rescue mission and caught his attention in the wilderness through the means of a burning bush and there he repeatedly referred to himself as 'the God of Abraham, the God of Isaac and the God of Jacob (Exodus 3:6, 16; 4:5). For a people lost and disorientated, far from their true place of belonging, this repeated reference to Abraham, Isaac and Jacob brought much comfort. It was to this father, son and grandson that God had made a covenant: he promised to build a community of faithful people, would provide them with a land to dwell in and would stick with them.

In the next two weeks, we will study the second character—Isaac. In some ways he is a more shadowy figure than his father or son. Abraham was the great founder, the one who heard the original call from God and got the whole story started. Jacob had many adventures and also fathered the twelve sons after whom the tribes of Israel are named. Then, in the middle, we have Isaac, who was born when Abraham and Sarah were elderly and was given the name 'laughter'. Despite the fact that he had to face a few traumatic experiences in childhood and adult life, you do get the sense that laughter was never too far from him. His laughter was not the raucous laughter of trivial jokes nor that of desperately trying to look on the bright side, but more the kind of laughter that rises above the varying circumstances of life and is rooted in the knowledge that, in the end, 'all things shall be well, and all manner of things shall be well', to quote Julian of Norwich. There was much that could have made Isaac quite depressed, but there is a steadfastness of soul in him that is evident in the stories that we shall be reading in the coming fortnight.

Michael Mitton

Sunday 7 October

GENESIS 17:15–17 (NRSV)

An unlikely promise

God said to Abraham, 'As for Sarai your wife, you shall not call her Sarai, but Sarah shall be her name. I will bless her, and moreover I will give you a son by her. I will bless her, and she shall give rise to nations; kings of peoples shall come from her.' Then Abraham fell on his face and laughed, and said to himself, 'Can a child be born to a man who is a hundred years old? Can Sarah, who is ninety years old, bear a child?'

Even though we find people living to a great age in the book of Genesis, we are clearly meant to understand that it is extraordinary for a man of 100 to father a child and a woman of 90 to bear that child. Despite being a great man of faith, Abraham's response to the news is to collapse in laughter. The whole idea is completely ludicrous. It is as if Abraham has a split personality at this point—there is his faithful self, who has heard the call of God and will follow him to the ends of the earth, and there is his 'rational' self, who is certain that women of 90 do not bear children! Any of us standing next to him would most likely say something to the effect of, 'Yes, Abraham, of course God does not mean this literally. That would be quite ridiculous—laughable, in fact!' but we would all be caught out by the serious look on God's face.

In the New Testament, Abraham is commended for his great faith (Romans 4:19) and, though he had his moment of doubt in this story, he recovers himself and shows that he is willing to trust God even if it seems ludicrously impossible. It is into this world of faith that Isaac is born and it has its effect on him. Faith is infectious and it is a good discipline to spend time with people with attractive faith, so that when our turn comes for God to speak 'impossibilities' to us, we laugh with faith, not with doubt.

Reflection

Who or what causes faith to grow in you?

MICHAEL MITTON

Genesis 18:12–15 (NRSV)

Laugh out loud

Sarah laughed to herself, saying, 'After I have grown old, and my husband is old, shall I have pleasure?' The Lord said to Abraham, 'Why did Sarah laugh, and say, "Shall I indeed bear a child, now that I am old?" Is anything too wonderful for the Lord? At the set time I will return to you, in due season, and Sarah shall have a son.' But Sarah denied, saying, 'I did not laugh'; for she was afraid. He said, 'Oh yes, you did laugh.'

I can imagine that Sarah would have preferred this story be omitted from the text as her unbelief is all too clear to see. I am pleased it is there, though, because it tells us that these heroes of faith are essentially as human as the rest of us. Laughter reverberates around the stories of the conception and birth of Isaac. When he is born to the 91-year-old Sarah, she proclaims, 'God has brought laughter for me; everyone who hears will laugh with me' (21:6). Indeed, those reading (or hearing) the story in the original Hebrew would not miss the fact that the name Isaac is based on the word 'laughter'. The laughter of disbelief becomes the laughter of faith—delighted laughter at the fact there is a God in the universe who does things that are utterly wonderful.

To some extent this might have helped the young Isaac as he grew up with parents who were old enough to be great-grandparents, and I like to think that there was much laughter in the home. There are moments in Isaac's life where there is little to laugh about, but the theme of laughter had been impressed on his soul from his conception. I think it is something significant that, in the middle of that great trio of Abraham, Isaac and Jacob, there is laughter. In a world with so much to dampen our spirits, it is good to be reminded that, in the roots of our faith stories, we have this theme of bubbling laughter asking, 'But is anything too wonderful for the Lord?'

Prayer

God of wonders, let laughter be my companion today.

Michael Mitton

GENESIS 22:6–8 (NRSV)

The slopes of mystery

Abraham took the wood of the burnt offering and laid it on his son Isaac, and he himself carried the fire and the knife. So the two of them walked on together. Isaac said to his father Abraham, 'Father!' And he said, 'Here I am, my son.' He said, 'The fire and the wood are here, but where is the lamb for a burnt offering?' Abraham said, 'God himself will provide the lamb for a burnt offering, my son.' So the two of them walked on together.

We may know this story well and feel relief when God halts Abraham's knife at the very last minute (v. 11), but Isaac had no certainty about a last-minute reprieve. For Abraham, the whole experience is a test of his faith and loyalty to God, but for his son the experience must have been utterly bewildering and terrifying. We know that Abraham loves his son (v. 2) and Isaac trusts his father completely. As far as he is concerned, his father is taking him on a special journey for a special act of worship to the God they serve. We do not know what age he is in this story, but he is old enough to carry a supply of wood and, as he stumbles up the hill under the weight of it, he is aware that one crucial thing is missing—the lamb for the sacrifice. He is satisfied with his father's reply, that God will provide, and only Abraham knows the grim truth as to the identity of the victim.

What comes through in this part of the story is the touching love and trust between father and son. For Isaac, up until now, the faith displayed in the home has been full of light and laughter, but the time has come for him to learn that there is a mysterious side to God's character and it is Abraham's task to introduce this side of God to his son. A faith that is all light and laughter will always be limited. There are moments in life when we have to climb the slopes of the mystery of God.

Reflection

What has helped you when you have had to face the mysterious workings of God?

MICHAEL MITTON

GENESIS 22:10–12 (NRSV)

The fear of God

> Then Abraham reached out his hand and took the knife to kill his son. But the angel of the Lord called to him from heaven, and said, 'Abraham, Abraham!' And he said, 'Here I am.' He said, 'Do not lay your hand on the boy or do anything to him; for now I know that you fear God, since you have not withheld your son, your only son, from me.'

Isaac watches the old man arrange the wood, still wondering where the lamb is for the sacrifice until his broken-hearted father turns to him and, with shaking hands, binds him with rope. The awful truth is now out—he is to be the sacrifice. He must surely have been petrified as Abraham tightened the bonds around him and laid him down on the wood. He may well have had the strength to fight his father off, but perhaps he submitted to his will, dreadful though it was. Then a voice from heaven called out and Abraham, with great relief, used the knife not to sacrifice his son, but set him free. The voice from heaven says that the reprieve has come because Abraham has proved that he fears God. Happily there is a ram caught in the thicket that can serve as the sacrifice.

Quite what Isaac made of the whole business, we do not know, but it must have had a profound influence on him for the rest of his life. He now knew that this God his father chose to follow meant business and the life of faith was not just a hobby but a matter of life and death. He also learned something about what it meant to fear God, which, he discovered, turned out to be nothing to do with feeling fearful of him, but more about loving him beyond anything else or anyone else in the world. Sometimes disturbing things happen in life that give us an opportunity to reflect on just how much we love God and how willing we are to follow him.

Reflection

What does the 'fear of God' mean to you?

MICHAEL MITTON

GENESIS 22:15–18 (NRSV)

The heart that hears

> The angel of the Lord called to Abraham a second time from heaven, and said, 'By myself I have sworn, says the Lord: Because you have done this, and have not withheld your son, your only son, I will indeed bless you, and I will make your offspring as numerous as the stars of heaven and as the sand that is on the seashore. And your offspring shall possess the gate of their enemies, and by your offspring shall all the nations of the earth gain blessing for themselves, because you have obeyed my voice.'

Abraham and Isaac watch the fire blaze, both of them still full of gratitude that it is not Isaac's body being cremated. Abraham calls the place 'The Lord will provide' (v. 14), for it had been sanctified by the presence of God (signified by his voice speaking to Abraham). This would be a hallowed place for generations to come and the story would be told again and again. The father and son now turn to start their journey home, but the voice speaks for a second time and they are stopped in their tracks. The voice of God addresses Abraham, presumably in Isaac's hearing, and what Isaac hears is that not only will their descendants be too numerous to count but also, because of this act of obedience, these descendants will have victory over their enemies and all the nations of the earth will find blessing.

The emotional journey for Isaac is extraordinary. One moment he is strapped to a funeral pyre, waiting for his father to bring his life to an untimely end, and the next he is hearing that he will have descendants who will change the face of the earth. Walking back down that hillside, he must have mulled over all of this very carefully and discussed it with his wise and faith-filled father. He learned that Abraham's act of obedience enabled him to be open to revelation. We all long to hear God's voice and seek his direction and, among other things, this story teaches us that openness to hearing God comes through faithful obedience.

Prayer

Grant me an obedient heart, O Lord, that I may hear your voice.

MICHAEL MITTON

GENESIS 24:45–47 (NRSV, ABRIDGED)

Introducing Rebekah

[Abraham's servant said] 'Before I had finished speaking in my heart, there was Rebekah coming out with her water-jar on her shoulder; and she went down to the spring, and drew. I said to her, "Please let me drink."... So I drank, and she also watered the camels. Then I asked her, "Whose daughter are you?" She said, "The daughter of Bethuel, Nahor's son, whom Milcah bore to him." So I put the ring on her nose, and the bracelets on her arms.'

Isaac knows that he will have many descendants, but as yet he does not know through whom he will have them. After Sarah dies (23:2), Abraham decides it is time for Isaac to find a wife and, in Genesis 24, we have a long and involved story describing how Abraham sets about finding this wife. He does so by sending the senior servant of his household back to the land of his ancestors. The servant heads off and, outside the city of Nahor, he rests by a well and notices some women coming to collect water. He prays that God will identify Isaac's future wife by her offering to provide water for his camels (vv. 11–14). Today's passage is part of the story reported by the servant, who tells us that Rebekah was the young woman thus identified as Isaac's wife. The family agrees to the betrothal and the servant brings Rebekah back to Isaac. The final line in this chapter tells us that Rebekah became Isaac's wife, 'and he loved her. So Isaac was comforted after his mother's death' (v. 67).

The role of the servant in this story, therefore, is crucial. We do not know his name, although he may well be the Eliezer mentioned in chapter 15, who was Abraham's right-hand man. The story centres on the relationship between Isaac and Rebekah, but it is the servant who is the hero and displays trust in God. There are times in life when we may feel that we are on the edge of things, a minor part in the story, yet, in God's plan, the part we play may be crucial.

Reflection

God has plans to be worked out in his world today.
What is your part in them?

MICHAEL MITTON

GENESIS 25:8–11 (NRSV)

Abraham's burial

> Abraham breathed his last and died in a good old age, an old man and full of years, and was gathered to his people. His sons Isaac and Ishmael buried him in the cave of Machpelah, in the field of Ephron son of Zohar the Hittite, east of Mamre, the field that Abraham purchased from the Hittites. There Abraham was buried, with his wife Sarah. After the death of Abraham God blessed his son Isaac. And Isaac settled at Beer-lahai-roi.

So Abraham finally dies. He is a man 'full of years' (175 of them, according to verse 7). There is only a brief report of his death, telling us where he was buried and that he rested with his beloved Sarah. Word must have got to Ishmael, for he returns to join his brother in burying their father. Ishmael was the firstborn son of Abraham by Hagar, the Egyptian handmaid of Sarah (16:15), but things were far from comfortable between Sarah and Hagar (vv. 4–6) and, when Isaac was born, the jealousies and anxieties increased. Sarah eventually instructed Abraham to send Hagar and Ishmael far away into the desert, where Ishmael, in time, married an Egyptian woman (21:8–20). As the story is related, there was clearly bitterness between the two branches of the family, but it is good to discover that peace seems to have been restored between the two half-brothers when Abraham died.

The writer of today's passage tells us that God blessed Isaac as he settled in Beer-lahai-roi, a place linked with an earlier Ishmael story (16:14). Isaac now focuses on the future, possibly deliberately leaving old family feuds behind him. He moves on in his life, aware of the promises that have to be fulfilled through him. The burial of his and Ishmael's father is a time also for them to bury the hatchet. Times of emotional vulnerability can cause us to review what is really valuable in life and decide to heal the past and live better in the future.

Prayer

Lord, grant me an open heart to heal my past and bless my future.

MICHAEL MITTON

GENESIS 25:21, 24–26 (NRSV)

Hair and heels

> Isaac prayed to the Lord for his wife, because she was barren; and the Lord granted his prayer, and his wife Rebekah conceived... When her time to give birth was at hand, there were twins in her womb. The first came out red, all his body like a hairy mantle; so they named him Esau. Afterwards his brother came out, with his hand gripping Esau's heel; so he was named Jacob. Isaac was sixty years old when she bore them.

As Isaac and Rebekah grew older, they must have been getting concerned at the lack of children coming along. There is a sense of history repeating itself, because Sarah and Abraham were unable to have children. Isaac, however, would have been steadfast in the knowledge that God had promised offspring and known that God was quite capable of performing miracles in this department. Perhaps it did not come as a great surprise, then, when Rebekah finally conceived. She discovers that she is bearing twins and is very aware of the babies struggling with each other before they are born (v. 22). She does the sensible thing, which is to listen to God about it. He tells her that there are two national leaders in her womb and the younger will lead the older (v. 23).

Isaac and Rebekah decide to name them according to their appearance at birth—Esau (meaning 'hairy') and Jacob (meaning 'grasping the heel', which also has the sense of 'deceiver')—and they certainly prove to be as different as chalk and cheese. There must have been moments when Isaac wondered how on earth the blessings God had promised were going to be delivered through these sons. Esau seemed interested mainly in his own belly and Jacob, fuelled by his mother's ambitions, grasped whatever heels he could find to gain more power. You get the sense, though, that Isaac rests in the knowledge that God can still work his purposes out despite the mix of foolishness, greed and jealousy in his household. It is a comfort to know God's blessings can be released in the muddle of human ambitions and failings.

Reflection

Think about times when you have seen God's plans worked out despite human failings.

MICHAEL MITTON

GENESIS 26:1–3 (NRSV)

In a foreign land

Now there was a famine in the land, besides the former famine that had occurred in the days of Abraham. And Isaac went to Gerar, to King Abimelech of the Philistines. The Lord appeared to Isaac and said, 'Do not go down to Egypt; settle in the land that I shall show you. Reside in this land as an alien, and I will be with you, and will bless you; for to you and to your descendants I will give all these lands, and I will fulfil the oath that I swore to your father Abraham.'

Isaac's story is not written in chronological order, so we now go back in time before the birth of the twins. Chapter 26 is a mosaic of stories about Isaac, the first of which is to do with a famine. Isaac is given specific instructions by God to go to Gerar, which was on the edge of Philistine territory, and also a place once visited by Abraham and Sarah (Genesis 20).

Here, history repeats itself, for Isaac becomes nervous about what will happen to Rebekah. He worries that because she is so beautiful, some men might kill him in order to take her, so he passes her off as his sister. Abraham followed the same device with Sarah on two separate occasions (Genesis 12:10–20 and 20:2–18). Although Isaac's deceit is discovered, it is not disastrous, however.

Isaac settles for a time in this foreign land and learns that God's presence is not confined to his homeland. The promise in verse 3 is 'reside in this land as an alien, and I will be with you'. Gerar becomes a kind of training ground for Isaac, for him to learn to trust in and experience the presence of God in a most unlikely place.

From time to time, God moves us, too, out of our comfort zones, into situations and places that feel alien. It may be a new church, a new town, a new job, new circumstances—all of these can be opportunities to discover the presence and blessing of God in new and unexpected ways.

Prayer

Lord, when I find myself in unfamiliar places,
teach me to discover your presence.

MICHAEL MITTON

GENESIS 26:23–25 (NRSV)

Wells of blessing

From there [Isaac] went up to Beersheba. And that very night the Lord appeared to him and said, 'I am the God of your father Abraham; do not be afraid, for I am with you and will bless you and make your offspring numerous for my servant Abraham's sake.' So he built an altar there, called on the name of the Lord, and pitched his tent there. And there Isaac's servants dug a well.

Isaac has to stay in the land of the Philistines for some time, so here we find him as one who is going to make the most of every opportunity while he is there. Throughout this chapter describing his stay in Gerar, a strong theme is God's blessing and Isaac seriously prospers (vv. 12–14). He develops an interest in the wells of this land and discovers that those dug by his father Abraham a generation earlier have been filled in by the Philistines, so he reopens them (vv. 15, 18). He also digs a few new wells and gives them names that relate to the stories of the wells (vv. 20–22, 33). Thus, Rehoboth (meaning 'room') is so-called because Isaac acknowledges that God has given them plenty of space (v. 22). In today's passage, God appears to Isaac a second time, assuring him of his presence and reasserting his promise of descendants. All in all, it is a very rich season for Isaac, in a land that he might have expected to be very inhospitable.

When the famine hits his homeland and he has to move, Isaac shows an impressive ability to trust God and not only manage in a difficult situation but also flourish, leaving this bit of Philistine land in a much better state than when he found it.

There are times in life when we feel we are in an inhospitable place, but this story tells us that not only can we discover God's presence can cause us to flourish in unexpected ways but also we can change the place for the better.

Reflection

In the place and situation in which you find yourself at the moment, what would be the equivalent of Isaac's digging of wells?

MICHAEL MITTON

GENESIS 27:1–4 (NRSV)

A time to bless

> When Isaac was old and his eyes were dim so that he could not see, he called his elder son Esau and said to him, 'My son'; and he answered, 'Here I am.' He said, 'See, I am old; I do not know the day of my death. Now then, take your weapons, your quiver and your bow, and go out to the field, and hunt game for me. Then prepare for me savoury food, such as I like, and bring it to me to eat, so that I may bless you before I die.'

We are coming to the evening of Isaac's life. He is old, his eyesight is failing and he needs to start making preparations for his final departure. One of these is to bless his son. As Esau is the elder son, he is the one to be blessed, although Isaac may well have mixed feelings about this son, who has been difficult (26:34–35). Isaac, however, has followed the call on him and his family as best he can and is determined to see the blessing pass on to the next generation. So, he asks his son to go and prepare a meal for him, for he wants to be as strong as possible for the imparting of this blessing. As the story unfolds, we see that the blessing involves Isaac prophesying over his son (27: 27–29). In years to come, the elderly Jacob does the same for his sons shortly before his death (Genesis 49). Central to the blessing, therefore, is listening for God's prophetic word.

As we shall see tomorrow, Isaac is terribly deceived by Rebekah and Jacob, but, even so, the blessing carries such power and authority that it cannot be changed.

This story is about a very particular situation, but it nonetheless reveals the power of blessing. Any of us can draw near to the presence of God, asking him to bless those we love and care for. In doing so, we need to note Isaac's listening and prophetic heart for the one for whom he was seeking God's blessing.

Prayer

Pray for God's blessing on someone you know today and listen to God for them.

MICHAEL MITTON

GENESIS 27:22–25 (NSRSV)

The tangled web

So Jacob went up to his father Isaac, who felt him and said, 'The voice is Jacob's voice, but the hands are the hands of Esau.' He did not recognise him, because his hands were hairy like his brother Esau's hands; so he blessed him. He said, 'Are you really my son Esau?' He answered, 'I am.' Then he said, 'Bring [the food] to me, that I may eat of my son's game and bless you.'

'Oh what a tangled web we weave, when first we practise to deceive' wrote Sir Walter Scott, and he might well have been writing about Jacob and Rebekah. Jacob has already bribed Esau out of his birthright, but now he and Rebekah trick Isaac into giving his blessing to Jacob. Here Jacob lives up to his name and succeeds in deceiving his own father, with the connivance of his mother. It is clear that Isaac has his suspicions (v. 21), but in the end he chooses to trust the voice that is speaking to him. Perhaps he finds it impossible to believe that his own son would deceive him in this way. While it is hard to commend Rebekah for her part in this story, it is just possible that she was trying to engineer the situation so that the most suitable son got the blessing and eventually Jacob does prove himself to be worthy of it. When Esau arrives on the scene and discovers the deception, he is understandably distraught and vows to kill his brother (v. 41).

It takes some time for Jacob to untangle the web of deceit he and his mother wove and it involves a night of struggling with God before he changes his nature and name. For moments in this story, Isaac must have been stunned and felt very foolish, but he shows extraordinary control as he blesses the real Esau. It is a mixed blessing for this son, for it promises emptiness and violence as well as eventual freedom (vv. 39–40). Perhaps in his old age, Isaac has learned that, in God's plans, nothing is a complete disaster—not even human deception.

Reflection

If you have been hurt by deception, how have you found healing?

MICHAEL MITTON

GENESIS 28:1–4 (NRSV)

Life moves on

Then Isaac called Jacob and blessed him, and charged him, 'You shall not marry one of the Canaanite women. Go at once to Paddan-aram to the house of Bethuel, your mother's father; and take as wife from there one of the daughters of Laban, your mother's brother. May God Almighty bless you and make you fruitful and numerous, that you may become a company of peoples. May he give to you the blessing of Abraham, to you and to your offspring with you, so that you may take possession of the land where you now live as an alien—land that God gave to Abraham.'

Life is far from easy for Isaac at this point. His health is failing, his eyesight is so poor that he cannot tell one son from the other, his beloved wife has deceived him, his younger son is running for his life and his older son is a hairy mass of fury and vengeance. He could have given up on the lot of them, but calls Jacob to him again, perhaps knowing that he and his son will be apart for many years. He knows Jacob has deceived him, but, despite that, the blessing has happened and Jacob now has to fulfil his responsibilities. Isaac's last instruction to his son is to tell him to find a wife from the right family, so that the plans of God can be fulfilled, the plans for a people and a land.

Isaac could have wallowed in self-pity and lamented the disappointing habits and faults of both his sons' and his wife's behaviour—he had been hurt by all of them—but he seems to have found a way of letting go of all of that. He is not preoccupied by the troubles of the present because, in his heart, he has become long-sighted. He is building for a future of which he will never be part, for his longing is for the purposes of God. When we are hit by troubles of any kind, it is good to think of this steady servant of God.

Prayer

Lord, when I am preoccupied with everyday troubles,
give me the long-sighted heart of Isaac.

MICHAEL MITTON

GENESIS 35:27–29 (NRSV)

Rest in peace

Jacob came to his father Isaac at Mamre, or Kiriath-arba (that is, Hebron), where Abraham and Isaac had resided as aliens. Now the days of Isaac were one hundred and eighty years. And Isaac breathed his last; he died and was gathered to his people, old and full of days; and his sons Esau and Jacob buried him.

After bidding Jacob farewell, Isaac steps to one side of his life for many years and disappears from the Genesis story for a time. His final appearance is in today's passage, which tells us that Jacob eventually came back to Isaac and they met at Mamre—the place where Abraham welcomed the three angelic visitors and was told that Sarah would give birth to Isaac and where she laughed in response (18:1–15).

As we come to the end of Isaac's life, we are therefore reminded of his beginning and the important connection with Abraham. Jacob would no doubt have told his old father of his first and second wives, twelve sons and a daughter. The wife he adored, however, Rachel, died in childbirth and no doubt old Isaac would have shared this sadness. He would also have sensed the change in Jacob, following the encounter with God at Jabbock, where he finally lost the 'deceiver' name and became 'Israel' (32:22–31).

Isaac would have been delighted to hear about the grandchildren and he would know that the promises the Lord had made to himself and his father Abraham were being fulfilled. He could rest content, knowing that the plans for the good land, filled with descendants as numerous as stars and sand, were well under way.

Thus, this man, full of days, faith and laughter, breathed his last. Just as Abraham's death brought his two estranged sons together for his burial, so Isaac's death does the same for Jacob and Esau. Bygones are bygones and they are free to move on into a future blessed by the God of Abraham, Isaac and Jacob.

Reflection

As you look back over the last two weeks, how has God been speaking to you through the stories of Isaac?

MICHAEL MITTON

Acts 15—20

When I was in my teens, I discovered an exciting paraphrase of the book of Acts. Prepared by J.B. Phillips, it was called *The Young Church in Action* (1955). As someone who had only recently discovered Christ, the title attracted me. I wanted to be part of what God was doing among young people in the church, too! At that time, the Holy Spirit was beginning to move in new ways and the life of the early church was attracting the attention of some of us who wanted to be followers of 'the Way', as Luke suggests Christianity was originally called (Acts 9:2). Since then, I have never lost my love for the book of Acts.

The book of Acts reflects all the new, fresh nature of the life of the early church. Yes, Jesus had been taken up into heaven, but then the Holy Spirit had come with power. Soon those first followers had the resources to do as Jesus had asked. The task was enormous—to go into all the world with his message.

So, the passages that we will take a look at in the next three weeks come from the very centre of the book of action! Here is action, indeed: God, men and women, believers, recent converts and non-believers, miracles and visions, amazing deliverances and scary tight corners. It is hardly surprising that J.B. Phillips is reported to have said that it all sounded a bit like rewiring a house without being able to turn the mains off.

Whether you think of yourself as young and active or feel you are not as much of either as you would like to be, here are things to consider. As always in *New Daylight*, each section ends with either a prayer or a reflection and these are designed to help you look at the particular angle we may have taken in approaching elements of the story. Two of us have shared the task of writing and, looking at the finished text of my contribution, I am struck by the diversity of prayers and reflections that have come out of the book of Acts. An amazing God and amazing people!

Heather Fenton

ACTS 15:1–2, 7, 19 (TNIV, ABRIDGED)

New beginnings

> Certain individuals came down from Judea to Antioch and were teaching the believers: 'Unless you are circumcised, according to the custom taught by Moses, you cannot be saved.'... Paul and Barnabas were appointed, along with some other believers, to go up to Jerusalem to see the apostles and elders about this question... After much discussion, Peter got up and addressed them: 'Brothers, you know that some time ago God made a choice among you that the Gentiles might hear from my lips the message of the gospel and believe... It is my judgment, therefore, that we should not make it difficult for the Gentiles who are turning to God.'

New beginnings can be fraught with problems. How much did the Jewish traditions matter? How should Gentile followers of the Way behave? This argument focused on whether or not non-Jewish believers should be circumcised. The believers in Antioch realised that this problem needed to be resolved by a wider group and sent Paul and Barnabas to Jerusalem to discuss it. On their way, they shared stories about new Gentile believers (v. 3), who may have helped them think further about this vexed question. After much discussion, the Jerusalem assembly decided that God was asking them not to make it difficult to become a member of the church. They were also helped in their decision by reflecting on Old Testament prophecy.

Although we tend to think of all this happening so long ago that it is probably not relevant, our world is, in some ways, similar to the multicultural world of the early church. As a result of the Roman infrastructure, communication between diverse groups was relatively easy. Therefore, just as now, diversity and cultural adaptation brought important issues into focus. The followers of Christ used prayer, experience, discussion and reflection on scripture to reach conclusions about what God was saying to them in their situation. We, too, need to ask ourselves in what ways God is challenging us today to make it easier for people to join the church, despite cultural differences.

Reflection

Is God saying anything to me personally or to my church about how to respond to situations in which we find ourselves at the moment?

HEATHER FENTON

ACTS 15:22–23, 28–35 (TNIV, ABRIDGED)

What does all this mean?

Then the apostles and elders, with the whole church, decided to choose some of their own men and send them to Antioch with Paul and Barnabas… With them they sent the following letter: '… It seemed good to the Holy Spirit and to us not to burden you with anything beyond the following requirements: You are to abstain from food sacrificed to idols, from blood, from the meat of strangled animals and from sexual immorality. You will do well to avoid these things… The people read it and were glad for its encouraging message. Judas and Silas, who themselves were prophets, said much to encourage and strengthen the believers… But Paul and Barnabas remained in Antioch, where they and many others taught and preached the word of the Lord.

The outcome of the discussions came back with some trusted individuals, so people knew that they had the approval of the church in Jerusalem. This, together with the words 'It seemed good to the Holy Spirit and to us' show that the message was authentic. The outcome? While not having to adhere to Jewish rites, the believers were told that there remained some expected standards of behaviour for them, to do with food and sexual morality. This message was well received and Paul and Barnabas decided to stay with the Antioch church for a while.

So, here we delve deeper into what it meant to be one of the very earliest Christian believers. The Jews had their traditions and needed to decide which they should keep. For the Gentile believers, there was now the challenge of following some instructions about how to live that might have been quite different from how they had behaved before. They may have thought it was normal to eat meat offered to idols or that had been strangled. If following Christ today no longer includes these questions about food, surely there are many issues for us to face—for example, about sexual behaviour. What is acceptable and what is not?

Prayer

Lord, whether we are new Christians or have sought to follow you for a long time, help us to know how to live in a way that honours your gospel.

HEATHER FENTON

ACTS 15:36–39; 16:1–5 (TNIV, ABRIDGED)

Just when it seemed to be going well!

Some time later Paul said to Barnabas, 'Let us go back and visit the believers in all the towns where we preached the word of the Lord...' Barnabas wanted to take John, also called Mark, with them, but Paul did not think it wise to take him, because he had deserted them in Pamphylia... They had such a sharp disagreement that they parted company... Paul came to Derbe and then to Lystra, where a disciple named Timothy lived... Paul wanted to take him along on the journey, so he circumcised him ..., As they travelled from town to town, they delivered the decisions reached by the apostles and elders in Jerusalem... So the churches were strengthened in the faith and grew daily in numbers.

So far we have seen decisions being made that were accepted by everyone. Some really prayerful listening had taken place and God's will was discerned. As often happens, however, after something really important, trouble followed. There was a row: Paul and Barnabas had decided to return to some towns and Barnabas wanted to take John Mark with them. Paul thought of John Mark as an unreliable person and did not want to work with him again. Their disagreement was so fierce that, in the end, they went their separate ways.

The writer of Acts chooses to follow Paul's travels and soon records him finding an alternative companion in the form of a man of mixed Greek and Jewish ancestry called Timothy. He ends up travelling with Paul, but only after he has been circumcised because local people would expect it, due to his mixed race background (16:1, 3). So, immediately, new considerations modify the decision that had been made!

Together, Paul and Timothy delivered 'the decisions reached by the apostles and elders in Jerusalem for the people to obey' (16:4). People were not put off by the rules; instead the church grew daily. This shows how we may need to be willing to modify decisions we have made, in the light of subsequent events. The eventual evidence of having taken care over such issues is God's blessing, in spite of earlier disagreements.

Reflection

When God shows us something important, a period may follow of trial and temptation, even disruption or disagreement.

HEATHER FENTON

ACTS 16:9, 12–15 (TNIV, ABRIDGED)

Come over and help us!

During the night Paul had a vision of a man of Macedonia standing and begging him, 'Come over to Macedonia and help us.'... We travelled to Philippi, a Roman colony and the leading city of that district of Macedonia. And we stayed there several days. On the Sabbath we went outside the city gate to the river, where we expected to find a place of prayer. We sat down and began to speak to the women who had gathered there. One of those listening was... named Lydia, a dealer in purple cloth. She was a worshipper of God. The Lord opened her heart to respond to Paul's message. When she and the members of her household were baptised, she invited us to her home.

Jesus had commissioned his disciples to 'be my witnesses to the ends of the earth' (Acts 1:8). The plans of Paul and his companions to visit the province of Asia were opposed by 'the Spirit of Jesus' (16:7) and now they responded to a vision bringing a call for help, presenting a whole new challenge. Having arrived in the region, they went to the leading Roman town of Philippi. In this province of Macedonia, women could hold higher social positions than in other provinces and, while speaking outside the city gates, they met Lydia—a dealer in fine cloth and also a worshipper of God. She was baptised and asked her new friends to stay with her.

Here is the beginning of a whole new phase of spreading the gospel. A supernatural vision, an obedient response and an element of common sense all interact. They were in the right place at the right time and soon they had some new converts, as well as accommodation in a merchant's house. Bringing together the everyday and the extraordinary, God worked a plan that was a seamless whole and yet more people were added to the young church.

Prayer

Lord, at times we can feel as if we are wandering round in darkness, confused and discouraged. Give us grace to recognise open doors and the courage to walk through them with a mixture of simple obedience and down-to-earth common sense.

HEATHER FENTON

ACTS 16:16–19, 23 (TNIV)

A turn for the worse?

> Once when we were going to the place of prayer, we were met by a female slave who had a spirit by which she predicted the future. She earned a great deal of money for her owners by fortune-telling. She followed Paul and the rest of us, shouting, 'These men are servants of the Most High God, who are telling you the way to be saved.' She kept this up for many days. Finally Paul became so annoyed that he turned round and said to the spirit, 'In the name of Jesus Christ I command you to come out of her!' At that moment the spirit left her. When her owners realised that their hope of making money was gone, they seized Paul and Silas... After they had been severely flogged, they were thrown into prison, and the jailer was commanded to guard them carefully.

Paul and Silas regularly visited the place of prayer, which was also frequented by a fortune-telling slave girl. She recognised them as 'servants of the Most High God' and you may have thought that her shouting about what they were doing would be helpful, but, in the end, Paul became so annoyed that he delivered her from whatever enabled her strange gift. Having lost their income, her owners found an excuse to get Paul and Silas into trouble (vv. 19–21). They were flogged and thrown into the local jail.

Where the gospel is proclaimed effectively, there will always be opposition. It may not immediately be apparent, but it will be there. It must have been pretty tiring to have had someone shouting about you all day and we see the humanity of Paul when, as we may have done, he loses his cool! Instead of improving things, however, the situation appears to get out of hand. The crowd takes the side of the people they see as victims and the unhappy preachers end up in the top security jail. They had to exchange Lydia's house for a dark cell, sitting with their feet in the stocks (v. 24).

Prayer

Lord, help me to be ready to follow where you are leading, whether it appears that it will be hard or easy.

HEATHER FENTON

ACTS 16:25–26, 29–35 (TNIV, ABRIDGED)

A welcome earthquake

About midnight Paul and Silas were praying and singing hymns to God, and the other prisoners were listening to them. Suddenly there was such a violent earthquake that the foundations of the prison were shaken. At once all the prison doors flew open, and everyone's chains came loose… The jailer called for lights, rushed in and fell trembling before Paul and Silas… and asked, 'Sirs, what must I do to be saved?'… Then they spoke the word of the Lord to him and to all the others in his house. At that hour of the night the jailer took them and washed their wounds; then immediately he and all his household were baptised… When it was daylight, the magistrates sent their officers to the jailer with the order: 'Release those men.'

Despite having received a severe flogging, Paul and Silus sit with their feet in chains, singing God's praises. Talk about being ready for anything! God has yet another plan, however—this time a 'natural phenomenon', happening at the right time and place. The jailer is rightly terrified, wondering who these men are and, as a result, before dawn breaks, is the latest addition to the Church. After his baptism, the two get a square meal, but, in later verses, we read that they are still looking for justice from the magistrates for illegally flogging two Roman citizens (vv. 37–39). Eventually they are politely escorted out of the city, but the incident brings to an end the superior accommodation they enjoyed at Lydia's house. They are back on the road again.

The flogging must have really hurt, yet the praises of God were so deep in these men's hearts that they could not help but sing. They praise God even before he acts to rescue them. Perhaps God spoke to the jailer through the singing as well as the terror of the earthquake. Although Paul is determined to complain about the illegal flogging, he also sees that it is time to move on. So here is another mixture of the miraculous, the political and the practical—and some more conversions.

Reflection

Following God's plan certainly has its ups and downs!
Are we ready for anything?

HEATHER FENTON

ACTS 17:1–7 (TNIV, ABRIDGED)

Trouble at Thessalonica

> Paul and his companions... came to Thessalonica... As was his custom, Paul went into the synagogue, and on three sabbath days he reasoned with them from the scriptures, explaining and proving that the Messiah had to suffer and rise from the dead... Some of the Jews were persuaded and joined Paul and Silas, as did a large number of God-fearing Greeks and not a few prominent women. But [others] were jealous; so they rounded up some bad characters from the marketplace, formed a mob and started a riot in the city... They dragged Jason and some other believers before the city officials, shouting: 'These men who have caused trouble all over the world have now come here, and Jason has welcomed them into his house. They are all defying Caesar's decrees.'

This time the scene begins in the synagogue, where, for three Saturdays running, Paul goes to explain about Jesus being the Messiah. Some receive the message with gladness, others are jealous. I find it hard to imagine what there was to be jealous of, unless it was meeting people whose faith seemed more alive than theirs.

By this time, Paul and Silus have celebrity status: 'these men who have caused trouble over the world have come here' (v. 6). That is a bit of an exaggeration, but the complainers are obviously not impressed by meeting such famous people. Jason, one of the believers who has given them hospitality, ends up paying a high price for his kindness.

Politically, too, we see a shift in loyalties. The jealous people, who are unlikely to be impressed by decrees from Caesar, suddenly claim to be worried about such things. The other synagogue members, with the possible exception of Jason (if he was indeed a member), appear to have stayed silent throughout. Jealousy is a dangerous thing, whether the causes seem justified or not. Here are people who should have known better, although I suppose 'you shall not covet your neighbour's fame' is a bit of a leap from coveting his ox!

Prayer

Lord, in a world full of 'celebs' and advertisements for so much that seems so attractive, help me not to be jealous but keep my focus on serving you.

HEATHER FENTON

ACTS 17:10–15 (TNIV)

More trouble

As soon as it was night, the believers sent Paul and Silas away to Berea. On arriving there, they went to the Jewish synagogue. Now the Berean Jews were of more noble character than those in Thessalonica, for they received the message with great eagerness and examined the scriptures every day to see if what Paul said was true. Many of them believed, as did also a number of prominent Greek women and many Greek men. But when the Jews in Thessalonica learned that Paul was preaching the word of God at Berea, some of them went there too, agitating the crowds and stirring them up. The believers immediately sent Paul to the coast, but Silas and Timothy stayed in Berea. Those who escorted Paul brought him to Athens and then left with instructions for Silas and Timothy to join him.

Paul and Silas have moved on, this time to Berea. In the synagogue there, they receive a great welcome, with members spending time every day examining the scriptures 'to see if what Paul said was true' (v. 11). How refreshing to the spirit this must have been for the travellers, who, by this time, may have been longing for some peace and quiet. Trouble is never far away, however, and although they may not have had the convenience of mobile phones, news could still certainly travel. Before long, the people they thought had been left behind in Thessalonica were there, too, stirring up trouble again. Paul left immediately, so maybe he was the focus of their attention.

How exhausting it must all have been. They may have begun to feel that a pattern was setting in, of openness and acceptance turning to suspicion and questioning. Offence was caused and the end result was something unpleasant or illegal or both. It must have been lovely to help people understand about Jesus from what we call the Old Testament scriptures, but how sad that, after such a good start, the new believers had to be left to fend for themselves so soon.

Reflection

Some Christians face a constant threat of persecution for their faith. For them, a faithful life is lived at great cost. Hold these people out to the Lord in prayer.

HEATHER FENTON

ACTS 17:16–19, 22–23 (TNIV, ABRIDGED)

And so to Athens

While Paul was waiting... in Athens, he was greatly distressed to see that the city was full of idols. So he reasoned in the synagogue with both Jews and God-fearing Greeks, as well as in the market-place day by day... A group of Epicurean and Stoic philosophers began to debate with him... [They] brought him to a meeting of the Areopagus, where they said to him, 'May we know what this new teaching is that you are presenting?...' [Paul] said: 'People of Athens! I see that in every way you are very religious. For as I walked around... I even found an altar with this inscription: TO AN UNKNOWN GOD. So you are ignorant of the very thing you worship—and this is what I am going to proclaim to you.'

Paul was alone in Athens and wandered round, looking at the many religious sites there. He also listened to what was being discussed in the streets and took the opportunity to preach the gospel. He recognised that he needed to start with what people understood, so he began with the altar he saw dedicated 'to an unknown God'. The Greeks believed in many gods, so, probably on the basis that they may have missed one and caused offence, they had this made, just in case.

Almost anything was up for discussion among the Athenians and they were curious about Paul's new ideas. His exploration as a tourist had given him clues about how to start explaining. His hearers were probably expecting a speculative discussion, but Paul said he would tell them what they needed to know!

Finding opportunities to talk to people about our faith is important. It is good to start from where they are and, to do that, we probably need to listen to learn how they see the world. At the same time, as Christians, we should not be ashamed or distracted from pointing clearly to Christ.

Prayer

Thank you, Lord, that Paul took time to look and listen, so that he could speak in a way his listeners could understand. Help me to see opportunities to talk about you in this way, too.

HEATHER FENTON

ACTS 17:24–27, 30–34 (TNIV, ABRIDGED)

God is...

[Paul said] 'The God who made the world and everything in it is the Lord of heaven and earth and does not live in temples built by hands... Rather, he himself gives everyone life and breath and everything else... God did this so that they would seek him and perhaps reach out for him and find him, though he is not far from any one of us... Now he commands all people everywhere to repent. For he has set a day when he will judge the world with justice by the man he has appointed. He has given proof of this to everyone by raising him from the dead.' When they heard about the resurrection of the dead, some of them sneered, but others said, 'We want to hear you again on this subject.' At that, Paul left the Council. Some of the people became followers of Paul and believed.

Paul said that what Athens had was not enough. The temples were human handiwork; the whole world was God's! They ought to look for this great God, come to him in repentance and worship the One he sent into the world and resurrected from the dead. This news fascinated the Athenians and got them thinking. As elsewhere, some thought the message rubbish, but a few became believers. Paul used his time well while waiting for his companions.

Paul told them that 'we live and move and have our being' in God (v. 28). God is not just an idea and not just located in one place, never mind a religious place. God is everywhere, so God is here. He wants us to turn to him, love him, discover Jesus more fully.

The Athenians had only just begun to discover this wonderful truth. As Christians, we should not think of God as located in a particular place or even present only at a specific time (such as in church on Sunday mornings). The idea of living and moving in him is so much more exciting and dynamic.

Reflection

The idea of living and moving in God is amazing. With the psalmist we can say 'Where can I flee from your presence?' (Psalm 139:7)

HEATHER FENTON

ACTS 18:1–4 (NRSV)

People like us

After this Paul left Athens and went to Corinth. There he found a Jew named Aquila, a native of Pontus, who had recently come from Italy with his wife Priscilla, because Claudius had ordered all Jews to leave Rome. Paul went to see them, and, because he was of the same trade, he stayed with them, and they worked together—by trade they were tentmakers. Every sabbath he would argue in the synagogue and would try to convince Jews and Greeks.

One thing that delights me about women's ministry in the church is that I can now see 'someone like me' up at the front helping me to worship—after decades of seeing 'someone unlike me'. It makes all the difference to how included I feel. Paul also sought out people like himself with whom to settle for much of his long stay in Corinth.

We do not know whether Aquila and Priscilla were already Christians or not when he went to stay with them, but it seems likely as they do not appear to have had any objection to a Jewish Christian staying with them. Indeed, they may have been thrilled to have this prominent convert, who was already gaining a name in the Church, living at their house. (Incidentally, this is one of only two places where Aquila is mentioned first; in all other references, Priscilla is the leading name.)

From Paul's side, the important thing was that they were in the same 'day job' as him. For self-employed people, like Paul and like me, working life can be quite lonely. It must have been pleasant for Paul to work alongside this couple and perhaps chat about Christian theology as they did so. Later in Acts, we see Paul taking some allowable pride in the fact that he did not depend financially on the congregations he served (20:33–34).

Paul, however, does not only stay comfortably with people he has something in common with: he preaches to 'Jews and Greeks'. Cross-cultural mission is harder than working with 'your own kind', but it has created the worldwide Church we have now.

Reflection

What have you learned from people very unlike yourself?

VERONICA ZUNDEL

ACTS 18:12–15 (NRSV)

Church and state

> But when Gallio was proconsul of Achaia, the Jews made a united attack on Paul and brought him before the tribunal. They said, 'This man is persuading people to worship God in ways that are contrary to the law.' Just as Paul was about to speak, Gallio said to the Jews, 'If it were a matter of crime or serious villainy, I would be justified in accepting the complaint of you Jews; but since it is a matter of questions about words and names and your own law, see to it yourselves; I do not wish to be a judge of these matters.'

You can almost hear Proconsul Gallio sighing at these troublesome Jews who insist on bringing religious matters to him. Roman policy was to allow conquered peoples to continue to practise their own religion undisturbed, unless it conflicted with their loyalty to the emperor.

For Gallio, this is all a matter of 'words and names'. What does it matter in whose name the Jews worship? For traditional Jews, however, this new 'Jesus sect' is highly disturbing and threatens all they have held most dear.

Luke, the author of Acts, was a Gentile, and 'the Jews' don't come off very well in his second book. Sadly this can only too easily be used to fuel anti-Semitism—even though Jesus himself was a Jew. We should have some sympathy for these religious leaders who want the state to intervene on their behalf. They are fearful of new ideas in their faith, a faith they have clung to through exile, war and foreign occupation. (Ironically, this happens just when Paul has given up on the synagogue: see verse 6.)

Yet, Anabaptists, like me, believe that Gallio was right—the state should have no say in matters of faith. When Christianity became a state religion in its fourth century, it spread the faith around the world, but it also allied the church with worldly power and values and forced underground the anti-war stance that the church had taken until then. The state can foster religious freedom, but problems begin when it tries to enforce religious practice.

Reflection

What relationship should Christians have to politics?
Can you discuss this in a group?

VERONICA ZUNDEL

ACTS 18:24–26 (NRSV)

Tell me more

Now there came to Ephesus a Jew named Apollos, a native of Alexandria. He was an eloquent man, well-versed in the scriptures. He had been instructed in the Way of the Lord; and he spoke with burning enthusiasm and taught accurately the things concerning Jesus, though he knew only the baptism of John. He began to speak boldly in the synagogue; but when Priscilla and Aquila heard him, they took him aside and explained the Way of God to him more accurately.

What do you do when someone with 'burning enthusiasm' for the gospel arrives at your church? If it is small, like mine, you probably jump with joy and quickly recruit him or her to help with evangelism. What, though, if you have some questions about the depth or breadth of their understanding of the good news?

Some churches might quietly remove Apollos from ministry, but Priscilla and Aquila tactfully 'took him aside' and told him more about the way of discipleship. It is possible that they rebaptised him as well, for if he 'knew only the baptism of John', it may be that he was still relying on his own powers (which were clearly great) in his ministry. He needed to know what it meant to be baptised 'with the Holy Spirit and fire' (Matthew 3:11).

Jesus himself did not baptise anyone. He instructed his disciples, however, to 'make disciples… baptising them in the name of the Father and of the Son and of the Holy Spirit' (28:19). To serve God, we need to be 'filled with all the fullness of God' (Ephesians 3:19), as Jesus was (Colossians 1:19). Perhaps part of what Priscilla and Aquila taught Apollos is that our mission to the world is, first of all, God's mission; our calling is to see where God is at work and join in.

Reflection

The couple who founded my congregation, whom I often see as a modern 'Priscilla and Aquila', have a sign they hold up when they give talks. On one side it says 'What are you doing?' and on the other 'How can I help you?' They suggest we hear these as questions from God to us and ask them of God.

VERONICA ZUNDEL

Saturday 3 November

ACTS 19:1–6 (NRSV, ABRIDGED)

God in my middle

While Apollos was in Corinth, Paul... came to Ephesus, where he found some disciples. He said to them, 'Did you receive the Holy Spirit when you became believers?' They replied, 'No, we have not even heard that there is a Holy Spirit.' Then he said, 'Into what then were you baptised?' They answered, 'Into John's baptism.' Paul said, 'John baptised with the baptism of repentance, telling the people to believe in the one who was to come after him, that is, in Jesus.' On hearing this, they were baptised in the name of the Lord Jesus. When Paul had laid his hands on them, the Holy Spirit came upon them, and they spoke in tongues and prophesied.

Just before I went to university, I kept bumping into people who asked me, 'Are you baptised in the Holy Spirit?' I didn't like the implication that there was something lacking in my Christian life, but the prompts kept coming. Eventually, one evening at college, I gave in and said something like, 'OK, God, I really do not like this, but if there is something you want to give me, I will accept it.' Nothing happened at first, but the next morning my Bible reading was transformed and I was filled with overwhelming joy.

Of course the trials of life soon weighed me back down again. I still have doubts about the terminology of 'baptism in the Spirit' and the division it can cause, but I cannot deny that something happened and it was from God.

So, what are we to make of these Ephesian believers who 'have not even heard that there is a Holy Spirit'? Clearly, as for Apollos, there is something lacking in their experience of Jesus, but it is not a spiritual 'high' or impressive gift—it is Jesus' Spirit in us that enables us to live for him. I think what they are given through baptism in Jesus' name and the laying on of hands is what Anna describes in the popular book *Mister God, this is Anna* by 'Fynn' (1974): 'God is in my middle, and I am in the middle of God.'

Prayer

'As many of you as were baptised into Christ have clothed yourselves with Christ' (Galatians 3:27). Jesus, clothe me with yourself.

VERONICA ZUNDEL

ACTS 19:13–20 (NRSV, ABRIDGED)

Not in my name

Then some itinerant Jewish exorcists tried to use the name of the Lord Jesus over those who had evil spirits... Seven sons of a Jewish high priest named Sceva were doing this. But the evil spirit said to them... 'Jesus I know, and Paul I know; but who are you?' Then the man with the evil spirit leapt on them... and so overpowered them that they fled out of the house naked and wounded. When this became known to all residents of Ephesus, both Jews and Greeks, everyone was awestruck; and the name of the Lord Jesus was praised... A number of those who practised magic collected their books and burned them publicly... So the word of the Lord grew mightily and prevailed.

I cannot help laughing at what this evil spirit says to Sceva's sons. It sounds so like a typical Jewish joke! So what 'trick' were these would-be exorcists missing? Not a trick at all—I think they were trying to use the name of Jesus as a good luck charm. Jesus himself warned that 'Not everyone who says to me, "Lord, Lord," will enter the kingdom of heaven, but only one who does the will of my Father in heaven. On that day many will say to me, "Lord, Lord, did we not prophesy in your name, and cast out demons in your name, and do many deeds of power in your name?" Then I will declare to them, "I never knew you"' (Matthew 7:21–23). Jesus' name is not to be used, only to be praised, as the Ephesians go on to do.

Gallio thought the gospel was 'a matter of... words and names' (Acts 18:14). It is not; it is a matter of what our life is focused on. I am reminded of Jesus' parable of the two sons (Matthew 21:28–32)—one who told his father he would go and work in the vineyard, but did not do it and the other who said 'No' but later went and did the work. We know which son gained his father's approval.

Reflection

It is those who have the Spirit of Jesus, not those who repeat his name, who do God's will (2 Corinthians 3:5–6).

VERONICA ZUNDEL

ACTS 19:23–29 (NRSV, ABRIDGED)

Union trouble

About that time no little disturbance broke out concerning the Way... Demetrius, a silversmith who made silver shrines of Artemis, brought no little business to the artisans. These he gathered together... and said, 'Men, you know that we get our wealth from this business. You also see and hear that not only in Ephesus but in almost the whole of Asia this Paul has... drawn away a considerable number of people by saying that gods made with hands are not gods. And there is danger not only that this trade of ours may come into disrepute but also that the temple of the great goddess Artemis will be scorned...' When they heard this, they were enraged and shouted, 'Great is Artemis of the Ephesians!' The city was filled with the confusion.

As I write, friends of mine are demonstrating non-violently against the world's biggest arms fair, which sells arms and 'security equipment' to some of the world's most repressive regimes. There is a good case for saying that 'security', understood in military terms, is an idol of our times, as the famous statue of Artemis was an idol for Ephesus. It is also a profitable livelihood for some, as was the trade in silver portable shrines to Artemis.

Paul's different set of values has, according to Demetrius, caused disruption and danger to the way of life of the whole of Asia, but Demetrius, of course, is right. The values of those who follow what was then called the Way do indeed threaten the core of Ephesian culture and the source of the city's wealth. Many Christians today are, and should be, a challenge to the institutions of worldly power, whether it be the arms trade or exploitative multi-national companies. We are meant to be out of step with society. 'Woe to you,' said Jesus in Luke's account of the Sermon on the Mount, 'when all speak well of you, for that is what their ancestors did to the false prophets' (Luke 6:26). A prophet's first commitment is to being unpopular, which is probably why there are not many prophets around—we all want to be liked!

Prayer

Jesus, help me to stand for your kingdom values,
even when they are unpopular.

VERONICA ZUNDEL

ACTS 19:35–41 (NRSV, ABRIDGED)

Speaking peace

> But when the town clerk had quietened the crowd, he said, 'Citizens of Ephesus, who... does not know that the city of the Ephesians is the temple-keeper of the great Artemis and of the statue that fell from heaven? Since these things cannot be denied, you ought to be quiet and do nothing rash... If therefore Demetrius and the artisans with him have a complaint against anyone, the courts are open, and there are proconsuls; let them bring charges there against one another... For we are in danger of being charged with rioting today, since there is no cause that we can give to justify this commotion.' When he had said this, he dismissed the assembly.

Riots are a real danger in some parts of our country, as we have seen within the last year or so. This town clerk, with his pacifying words, is something of a hero—and a contrast to Demetrius, who stirred up the trouble in thc first place.

The clerk reminds me a bit of Gamaliel, who says of the new 'Jesus movement', 'If this plan or this undertaking is of human origin, it will fail; but if it is of God, you will not be able to overthrow them' (Acts 5:38–39). He seems to be saying something similar: 'if Artemis is so great, her cult will soon triumph over this new way; and if not, you have the courts to resort to'.

When people disagree violently, how do you react? Do you get out of the way, join in the fight, try to speak calming words? I am afraid that when I saw four young men on our street beating a man with a fence-post to try and get his laptop, I did not speak very calming words. I shouted 'Oi, you lot, lay off!' I think the mother in me was reacting to these 'naughty boys'! It worked, however—they threw the post away and ran off, without the laptop.

Perhaps to be ready to 'speak peace' in situations of conflict, we have to practise first on mild disputes. Being town clerk was probably excellent for this.

Prayer

Prince of Peace, teach me 'the things that make for peace' (Luke 19:42).

VERONICA ZUNDEL

ACTS 20:1–6 (NRSV, ABRIDGED)

Supporting cast

> After the uproar had ceased, Paul sent for the disciples; and after encouraging them and saying farewell, he left for Macedonia. When he had gone through those regions and had given the believers much encouragement, he came to Greece, where he stayed for three months... He was accompanied by Sopater son of Pyrrhus from Beroea, by Aristarchus and Secundus from Thessalonica, by Gaius from Derbe, and by Timothy, as well as by Tychicus and Trophimus from Asia. They went ahead and were waiting for us in Troas; but we sailed from Philippi after the days of Unleavened Bread, and in five days we joined them in Troas, where we stayed for seven days.

If your eyes glaze over when you read a biblical list of names, you are not alone. Old Testament genealogies or lists of Paul's associates can seem dull and irrelevant, but we should not gloss over them. I notice three things about this list. First, Paul never made his marathon journeys alone. He was always accompanied by at least one other 'mission worker' and often by a crowd of supporters. If you are in church leadership, do you have a circle not of cronies, but of people who will both support you and hold you accountable? Even one is better than none.

Second, these helpers came from many different places, with different cultures. Is your church's leadership team diverse? Does it include men, women, black, white, able-bodied, disabled, younger, older? If not, why not? Is there anything you can do about it?

Third, we know nothing further about any of this list (except Timothy and Luke himself). Their calling was to be faithful, not famous. We cannot all be international speakers or successful writers. What we can do is serve God in whatever God has called us to, which may be simply supporting someone whose role involves greater prominence.

What did these supporters do afterwards? Maybe they just went back to serve their home churches (apart from Luke—he became a successful Christian writer!) Meanwhile, Paul travelled on as he was called to do.

Reflection

Paul gave 'the believers much encouragement'.
Can you encourage someone today?

VERONICA ZUNDEL

ACTS 20:7–12 (NRSV, ABRIDGED)

Dead boring?

On the first day of the week, when we met to break bread, Paul was holding a discussion with them; since he intended to leave the next day, he continued speaking until midnight... A young man named Eutychus, who was sitting in the window, began to sink off into a deep sleep while Paul talked still longer. Overcome by sleep, he fell to the ground three floors below and was picked up dead. But Paul went down, and bending over him took him in his arms, and said, 'Do not be alarmed, for his life is in him.' Then Paul went upstairs, and... continued to converse with them until dawn... Meanwhile they had taken the boy away alive and were not a little comforted.

Long sermons can be wearing (Adrian Plass measures them in wine gums), but they are not usually fatal! Actually, this meeting in Troas was really a discussion—church discussion groups are nothing new. Maybe Eutychus found it hard to join in or maybe he had just been up late the night before. Clearly Paul was so involved in the talk that he did not notice this young man's peril.

The story of the early church is full of astounding miracles. Even handkerchiefs touched by Paul (I hope they were clean ones!) healed people (19:12). We rarely encounter such miracles today and raising someone from the dead is something we definitely do not expect. For this reason, some Christians believe miracles were only meant for the early days, that they do not happen today, but I know enough people who have been inexplicably healed to disagree with them.

If it was not initially so tragic, this story would be quite funny. I am amused that after this near-fatal incident, Paul happily goes on talking! I notice also that others take the boy away—they were not going to risk a repeat performance.

Perhaps what this story can say to us is something about the balance of teaching and pastoral work in our churches. We should not be so focused on getting people to believe the right things that we fail to notice they are dying of loneliness or stress.

Prayer

Help us to care for each other's minds, spirits and bodies.

VERONICA ZUNDEL

Acts 20:17–24 (NRSV, abridged)

In step with the Spirit

From Miletus [Paul] sent a message to Ephesus, asking the elders of the church to meet him. When they came to him, he said to them: 'You yourselves know how I lived among you the entire time from the first day that I set foot in Asia, serving the Lord with all humility and with tears, enduring the trials that came to me... proclaiming the message to you and teaching you... And now, as a captive to the Spirit, I am on my way to Jerusalem, not knowing what will happen to me there... But I do not count my life of any value to myself, if only I may finish my course and the ministry that I received from the Lord Jesus.'

Acts 19:10 tells us that Paul spent over two years in Ephesus. It was a strategic spot from which to reach out over all of what was then called Asia. It may also be that, with the strength of the cult of Artemis in the city, Paul needed to stay for pastoral reasons, to build up the beleaguered minority of believers. They must have been precious to him.

In 19:21, however, we read that he then 'resolved in the Spirit' to go through Macedonia and Achaia, where he had formerly preached the gospel. This was to be a stopping point on his journey to Jerusalem, the heart of the church, then on to Rome, the heart of the empire. He was determined to both strengthen the impoverished 'mother' church and challenge the 'powers that be'.

'Resolved in the Spirit' reminds me of the conclusion of the Jerusalem council: 'it has seemed good to the Holy Spirit and to us' (15:28). It suggests a cooperation between our own spirits and the Holy Spirit and God not overriding our common sense except when strictly necessary!

Here, however, Paul also calls himself 'a captive of the Spirit'. I do not think this means a kind of imprisonment, but, rather, that he was 'captivated' by the Spirit who infused his faith and life.

Reflection

'You... know how I lived... enduring the trials that came to me' (Acts 20:18–19). What may be the 'trials' of Christian ministry today? Pray for church leaders everywhere.

Veronica Zundel

ACTS 20:25, 29–32, 36–38 (NRSV, ABRIDGED)

A sad farewell

[Paul said] 'And now I know that none of you, among whom I have gone about proclaiming the kingdom, will ever see my face again... I know that after I have gone, savage wolves will come in among you, not sparing the flock... Therefore be alert... And now I commend you to God and to the message of his grace... that is able to build you up and to give you the inheritance among all who are sanctified...' When he had finished speaking, he knelt down with them all and prayed. There was much weeping among them all; they embraced Paul and kissed him, grieving especially because of what he had said, that they would not see him again.

My church often has a high proportion of Americans and Canadians—people who have come to London for a few years to work or study. Just when we are getting really fond of them, the time comes for them to leave. We always give them a 'leaving service', where we sit in a circle and share memories of them and a 'leaving book' in which we paste tributes, funny stories, photos or even poems (we do the same for British people who move away, too, of course).

These can be tearful occasions, but we also know that they may come back to visit or we can cross the Atlantic to visit them. Paul had no such assurance. No wonder there was 'much weeping'. No 'stiff upper lip' about it here!

Last night I was wondering how Jesus knew (in the Matthew 7 passage I quoted on Sunday) that there would be 'fake followers'—people who claimed his name but did not live as he lived. Paul has similar prescience about how malicious people are going to infiltrate the congregations he has founded and disrupt them. As I once said when commenting on the story of Mary of Bethany anointing Jesus' feet (John 12), 'This shows that whatever one Christian does for God, another Christian is bound to come along and criticise it!' Our only recourse is to do as Paul did—commit ourselves and each other to God.

Prayer

Blest be the tie that binds our hearts in Christian love.

John Fawcett, 1782

VERONICA ZUNDEL

The valley of dry bones: Ezekiel

The valley of dry bones is one of those Bible passages whose fame eclipses its original context. It inspired the 'traditional spiritual song' Dem Bones (anatomy and Scripture lesson combined), as well as providing a haunting image for those seeking to bring words of Christian encouragement to a difficult situation.

The book of Ezekiel—where this vision falls in chapter 37—is not as widely read or quoted as (say) Isaiah. Interestingly, however, biblical studies lecturer Ernest Lucas describes Ezekiel as 'one of the most visual of the major Hebrew prophets in the presentation of his message… Some of the other prophets occasionally perform symbolic actions, but Ezekiel performs what amounts to "street theatre"' (*People's Bible Commentary: Ezekiel*, 2002). At times, the prophet literally acted out his message (such as the siege of Jerusalem in chapter 4) and the dry bones vision is one of a number that involve him being what we might call 'teleported' to a particular location where God wishes to speak to him. This includes the rather painful note of his being carried to Jerusalem by 'a lock of my head' (8:3)!

The context for Ezekiel's ministry was the exile, of which we learned more in the last issue of *New Daylight*. A quick reminder: after the death of Solomon, Israel split into the kingdom of Israel, with its capital Samaria, and Judah, centred on Jerusalem. The two kingdoms faced the perennial problems associated with being small states surrounded by superpowers. Israel was defeated by the Assyrian empire in 722/1BC, while Judah was finally overwhelmed by the Babylonians in 587/6BC. Defeat meant hordes of people being taken into captivity abroad and the devastation of their city.

The dry bones episode comes in the final section of Ezekiel (chapters 33—48), which brings messages of hope and restoration after many earlier oracles of warning and judgment. These messages culminate in a breathtaking vision of a restored Jerusalem, the very name of which will be 'The Lord is There' (48:35). It would seem that, even as news of the fall of the first Jerusalem reached the captives (33:21), God spoke to assure them that all was not lost.

Naomi Starkey

EZEKIEL 37:1–2 (NRSV)

Dried up

The hand of the Lord came upon me, and he brought me out by the spirit of the Lord and set me down in the middle of a valley; it was full of bones. He led me all round them; there were very many lying in the valley, and they were very dry.

One of the things I love about living in my particular bit of Wales is the hidden valleys. Driving through the countryside (or cycling if I am feeling energetic), I take a side turning and a whole new landscape unfolds, hidden from the main road by the green hills, with its own settlements, woods and water. The valley described in the passage today could not be more different from those landscapes. The impression is of a gulch, a deep valley formed by erosion that, if the eroding river is dried up, can be prone to flash floods. It sounds a dried-up, hostile, isolated place.

In this silent gulch—too deep for the wind to do more than whisper, far from any human habitation—the prophet's feet tread in among heaps of bones. Led by the 'spirit of the Lord', he walks through what looks like the site of a terrible battle or perhaps a massacre of unarmed civilians. Whatever happened did so so long ago that not only has all the clothing rotted away but also the very bones have been bleached completely dry.

Some would argue that any place where devastating loss of life occurred, especially if it involved betrayal or summary execution, retains a chilling atmosphere. Think, they would say, of Glencoe, Wounded Knee, Auschwitz, Nyarubuye. Miraculously, however, life does go on even after terrible atrocities. Survivors slowly and painfully pick up the pieces of their lives and begin the long journey towards some kind of normality. Ezekiel's valley, however, is empty of everything except the remains of the dead: there were no survivors to bury the bodies, mourning them and paying them due respect. There appears to be no hope of healing or any kind of restoration.

Reflection

Pause to remember before God those who have died in wars, whether in direct combat or as victims of 'collateral damage'. Remember, too, those who did not die but whose lives were scarred by those deaths.

NAOMI STARKEY

Ezekiel 37:3–6 (NRSV)

God knows how

He said to me, 'Mortal, can these bones live?' I answered, 'O Lord God, you know.' Then he said to me, 'Prophesy to these bones, and say to them: O dry bones, hear the word of the Lord. Thus says the Lord God to these bones: I will cause breath to enter you, and you shall live. I will lay sinews on you, and will cause flesh to come upon you, and cover you with skin, and put breath in you, and you shall live; and you shall know that I am the Lord.'

From the first moment of Ezekiel's calling to be a prophet, when he saw 'the appearance of the likeness of the glory of the Lord' (1:28), he had been subjected to a series of disturbing visions and supernatural encounters, whereby he received words from God for the exiled people. After the very public humiliation of enacting the siege of Jerusalem (an ordeal that cost him more than 14 months) and the orders to shave his hair and beard and eat an admittedly tasty scroll, he is now called upon to prophesy to dried-up bones in an eerie valley. At least nobody is watching...

To the Lord's challenge—'Can these bones live?'—the prophet makes a wise response. The obvious answer is, 'No, of course not', but Ezekiel is loyal to his faith in the one God, mightier than any foreign deity, whose power is not limited by territorial considerations.

We may face a situation—in our personal lives, at work, in our church—that seems insurmountably difficult. We may have taken a step of what we thought was obedience to God, only to find that everything appears to be unravelling and what we had thought was a right choice seems to be turning out to be a fatal error. In such situations, the wise course is to be like Ezekiel here and hold on to what we know of God and trust that if we continue to seek his way and follow his command, life will come even from death.

Reflection

'Then Job answered the Lord: "I know that you can do all things, and that no purpose of yours can be thwarted"' (Job 42:1–2).

Naomi Starkey

Tuesday 13 November

Ezekiel 37:7–8 (NRSV)

Seriously, can these bones live?

So I prophesied as I had been commanded; and as I prophesied, suddenly there was a noise, a rattling, and the bones came together, bone to its bone. I looked, and there were sinews on them, and flesh had come upon them, and skin had covered them; but there was no breath in them.

Obediently, Ezekiel speaks to the bones, telling them that the Lord Almighty will restore them to life, against every appearance to the contrary. Then comes that wonderfully dramatic word—'suddenly'—and the drama of the scene intensifies. First comes the noise—a rattling—and we imagine the prophet breaking off, scared out of his wits, looking this way and that as the source of the noise becomes apparent. The bones are moving. As the prophet watches (I think, open-mouthed), the bones are reconstituted into bodies. First, the sinews knit the bones together, then the flesh covers them and, finally, the skin grows over all and they are recognisably human bodies rather than human remains. They are still dead, though.

Does Ezekiel panic at this point? The first words of prophecy that the Lord had given him for these wretched bones, as we read yesterday, were 'I will cause breath to enter you, and you shall live'. He has prophesied and, lo, the job of resurrection is only half done. Again, the drama deepens, for does this then show that the Lord is not, in fact, quite so powerful after all?

Today's passage is a reminder that even if something looks good, it can still lack the breath of life. In Welsh, the word for 'spirit'/'Spirit' is *ysbryd*, while *ysbrydoliaeth* means 'inspiration'. Without the life-giving inspiration of the Spirit of God, our work, our relationships or our worship can feel as hopeless as somebody moving the limbs of a dead body and then shouting, 'Look! They're still alive!' In truth, there is no life and only an illusion that life could be possible, for, even if there is a body, how can breath return to that which drew its last breath many, many years before?

Reflection

'The spirit of God has made me, and the breath of the Almighty gives me life' (Job 33:4)

Naomi Starkey

EZEKIEL 37:9–10 (NRSV)

Gift and giver

> Then he said to me, 'Prophesy to the breath, prophesy, mortal, and say to the breath: Thus says the Lord God: Come from the four winds, O breath, and breathe upon these slain, that they may live.' I prophesied as he commanded me, and the breath came into them, and they lived, and stood on their feet, a vast multitude.

There is a wonderfully creepy engraving of this scene by the French artist Gustave Doré. It shows the prophet standing at a relatively safe distance, silhouetted by apocalyptic clouds as the skeletons literally pull themselves together and get to their feet.

Following on from yesterday's Welsh lesson (the language of heaven, or so I am told), today we can note that the Hebrew word *ruach* is used for three different English words in the passage here—'breath', 'wind' and also 'spirit'—making these verses rich with layers of meaning. The same word occurs in Genesis 1, when 'a wind from God' (NRSV) or 'the Spirit of God' (NIV) sweeps over the dark, precreation waters, and in Genesis 2 (v. 7), where God breathes into the man 'the breath of life'.

We may be tempted to envisage a kind of zombie army here, silently staring at the anxious prophet as he wonders what on earth will happen next. The dead are alive, however, not just undead, and they are a 'vast multitude'. The desolate gulch would surely now fill with noise. Perhaps there are shouts of recognition, astonished laughter and also tears as the newly resurrected multitude mingle among the rocks. We might wonder, too, if God provided clothing as well as breath!

While the Bible is no science textbook, it is absolutely clear that God is the life-giver for all. Whatever the exact mechanism by which the gift was first given, the source of it is the Lord Almighty, who is also our Heavenly Father. It is a gift that is terribly easy to take for granted until we find we risk losing it—or fear its loss for one we love. Today, let us recollect both gift and giver and give thanks.

Reflection

'How precious is your steadfast love, O God! … For with you is the fountain of life' (Psalm 36:7, 9).

NAOMI STARKEY

EZEKIEL 37:11 (NRSV)

He has heard them

Then he said to me, 'Mortal, these bones are the whole house of Israel. They say, "Our bones are dried up, and our hope is lost; we are cut off completely."'

Finally we come to the point of this prophecy, but, as Ernest Lucas points out, it has often been misunderstood: 'From early Christian times, both Christian and rabbinical commentators have tended to read it in terms of the bodily resurrection' (*PBC Ezekiel*). In fact, at that time, there was no concept of life after death. All the dead, righteous and unrighteous alike, were thought to end up in a shadowy region known as Sheol. While Ezekiel's vision is a reminder that the Lord is the giver of life, it is also intended to teach that life can come from death in a metaphorical, rather than literal, sense.

The 'whole house of Israel' feels itself dried up and dead; hope is gone. As mentioned in the Introduction, God's people had suffered the fate common to so many smaller countries that have the misfortune to be surrounded by empires. Both Israel and Judah were fought over, dominated and eventually swallowed up once they had wilfully distanced themselves from God's protection. Now they no longer dare even ask for divine help because they have been 'cut off completely', not only from the temple (the heart of their worshipping life) but from the promised land, which had been the centrepiece of the covenant. God is bigger than they thought (as tomorrow's reading will show). He has heard their despairing cries and will respond beyond expectation.

While few places manage to avoid conquest altogether, it is salutary to reflect on the fate of, for example, some Central European countries that have repeatedly found themselves the victims of conflicting major powers. Such troubled history can have an impact on a people's sense of identity and self-worth that can continue, for better or worse, down the centuries. While many of the exiles from Israel and Judah were eventually able to return home, the trauma of exile changed things for ever.

Reflection and prayer

Pray for refugees, those who work with them and anyone who feels, for whatever reason, exiled from home.

NAOMI STARKEY

EZEKIEL 37:12–14 (NRSV)

Up from the grave

> 'Therefore prophesy, and say to them, Thus says the Lord God: I am going to open your graves, and bring you up from your graves, O my people; and I will bring you back to the land of Israel. And you shall know that I am the Lord, when I open your graves, and bring you up from your graves, O my people. I will put my spirit within you, and you shall live, and I will place you on your own soil; then you shall know that I, the Lord, have spoken and will act, says the Lord.'

Now the Lord gives Ezekiel his orders: 'tell my people that I am coming for them'. They may be metaphorically dead and buried, but God will show that that is no obstacle to his plans. Just as dry bones can become living beings again, so God's people can and will be resurrected.

The imagery here is quite different from and far more moving than that in yesterday's passage. Instead of the grotesque rattling of reassembling skeletons, we can imagine somebody uncovering a mass grave. As the bodies are uncovered, they are gently lifted and placed beneath the sky. Then the one digging lays aside the shovel and leans over the bodies, one by one, and breathes on them. Then, because this breath is the breath of life, the dead, one by one, stir and snatch a lungful of air. Their eyes open and, behold, they are alive again.

The promise to God's people is not only of resurrection but also restoration to their own land. The English translation does not show that the same Hebrew word, '*adam*' (yes, as in Genesis' Adam), is used here for both the 'land' of Israel and 'soil'. This is a homecoming that involves reconnecting with a place once known intimately—the kind of knowledge that farmers and devout gardeners have.

God has spoken; God will act. What the people have to do is trust, and wait for the word to be fulfilled.

Reflection

'And the ransomed of the Lord shall return, and come to Zion with singing; everlasting joy shall be upon their heads; they shall obtain joy and gladness, and sorrow and sighing shall flee away' (Isaiah 35:10).

NAOMI STARKEY

DANIEL 9:17–19 (NRSV)

The right response

> [Daniel prayed] 'Now therefore, O our God, listen to the prayer of your servant and to his supplication, and for your own sake, Lord, let your face shine upon your desolated sanctuary. Incline your ear, O my God, and hear. Open your eyes and look at our desolation and the city that bears your name. We do not present our supplication before you on the ground of our righteousness, but on the ground of your great mercies. O Lord, hear; O Lord, forgive; O Lord, listen and act and do not delay! For your own sake, O my God, because your city and your people bear your name!'

Daniel's prayer (vv. 4–19) is made 'in the first year of Darius…, who became king over the realm of the Chaldeans' (v. 1). He has calculated that the 70 years allotted for 'the devastation of Jerusalem' (v. 2) are finished. It must therefore be time for the restoration foreseen by Ezekiel, among many other prophets. Even so, this prayer is made 'with fasting and sackcloth and ashes' (v. 3) and consists largely of repentance for the people's sins. Daniel understands all too well the unfaithfulness of Israel and Judah—but he also knows how unfathomable is the faithfulness of God.

God makes the first move to mend the broken relationship, but that does not absolve the people of responsibility. They must be mindful of his mercy and respond with due humility, even as the promises of return come closer to fulfilment. When they are back on their own soil, will they raise a 'harvest of righteousness' (James 3:18) or not?

While we can never deserve the grace that heaven lavishes on us, we should not be tempted to take it lightly either. God's desire is to see us transformed into the people he always intended us to be, fully fit for his purposes. That transformation is unlikely to be a quick, easy or painless process. Even so, I think we can safely assume that the prize will be worth the process.

Reflection

'A new heart I will give you… and I will remove from your body the heart of stone and give you a heart of flesh' (Ezekiel 36:26).

NAOMI STARKEY

To be a pilgrim

Being a pilgrim is the calling of Christ's disciples. As pilgrims, we live with the tension of 'already, but not yet' for, although we have our redemption through Jesus' sacrificial death on the cross, we do not yet inhabit our heavenly bodies. The reminders of our fallen nature surround us—the unrest of disaffected youth, spats between siblings, our own pride and arrogance—yet we see glimpses of God's glory every day—an awe-inspiring sunset, a grieving parent who reaches out to the friends of her dead son, a smile between strangers.

Living within the tension of being redeemed from our sins yet also still sinful reminds us of our pilgrim status. God, through his Son and Spirit, reaches out to us, calling us to be empowered by his grace, truth and love. Our journey involves responding, stepping forth each day as we claim our status as God's beloved and God's pilgrims.

Scripture is filled with examples of pilgrims. Often the heroes of our faith embarked on a physical journey, leaving the familiar to follow God's call. One example in the Old Testament is the Israelites' exile and journey to the promised land—and all the wandering in between. Before that, we read of Abram, who was called to leave his people and his country. In the New Testament, Jesus himself exemplifies the life of the pilgrim, not least through being born just after his travelling parents found shelter in what amounted to a cave.

This fortnight we will explore the concept of pilgrimage through some of the biblical characters who lived in a state of 'already, but not yet'. We will also mark the American day of Thanksgiving on 22 November, looking at the experience of the Pilgrims who left the 'old world' for the 'New World', for, although pilgrimage is usually the act of going to a special or holy place, sometimes it involves setting off across the world to an unknown destination. Perhaps this involves never returning to one's original home. Ultimately, we, as Christians, are all journeying towards a place that sets the gold standard for what 'home' really means—heaven.

Amy Boucher Pye

GENESIS 12:1–4 (NIV)

Go, and be blessed

The Lord had said to Abram, 'Go from your country, your people and your father's household to the land I will show you. I will make you into a great nation, and I will bless you; I will make your name great, and you will be a blessing. I will bless those who bless you, and whoever curses you I will curse; and all peoples on earth will be blessed through you.' So Abram went, as the Lord had told him; and Lot went with him.

Today's passage is one of the early instances in the Bible of God making a covenant with his people. God gives Abram and Sarai a big task—namely, to renounce their ties to their families, land and inheritance, while trusting that God will bless them.

At a human level, what God is asking seems incredible, especially as Sarai was unable to bear children (11:30). Thus, for Abram and Sarai, becoming pilgrims entails a huge amount of faith. Not only does Abram not have an heir, but, by leaving his family, he renounces his earthly inheritance. He will not be caring for elderly parents or passing on his household goods to the next generation. From the point of view of his new countrypeople, too, his identity will be that of a foreigner and stranger.

Reading on in Genesis, we see that Abraham and Sarah (as they become) heed God's call and, in turn, God fulfils his promise to make Abraham's name great and give him as many descendants as there are stars. God's blessings more than overcome the sacrifices he required of Abraham and Sarah, but he did ask them to make a very big step in faith.

God might not be asking us to leave our homes and lands, but, even if we stay in the places we were born, he seeks in us a pliable heart and a willingness to follow him. Whether we stay or go, we can live the paradox highlighted by Jim Elliot, the missionary murdered in 1956, in his journal: 'He is no fool who gives what he cannot keep to gain what he cannot lose.'

Reflection

'Let us hold unswervingly to the hope we profess, for he who promised is faithful' (Hebrews 10:23).

AMY BOUCHER PYE

NUMBERS 10:29–33 (NIV)

A change of heart

Now Moses said to Hobab son of Reuel the Midianite, Moses' father-in-law, 'We are setting out for the place about which the Lord said, "I will give it to you." Come with us and we will treat you well, for the Lord has promised good things to Israel.' He answered, 'No, I will not go; I am going back to my own land and my own people.' But Moses said, 'Please do not leave us. You know where we should camp in the wilderness, and you can be our eyes. If you come with us, we will share with you whatever good things the Lord gives us.' So they set out from the mountain of the Lord and travelled for three days. The ark of the covenant of the Lord went before them during those three days to find them a place to rest.

Hobab was Moses' brother-in-law and Moses here appeals to him to join them as the Israelites leave Mount Sinai for Canaan. At first, Hobab says no, as he wants to return to his people, but Moses pleads with him, knowing that he will be an asset in the wilderness.

The biblical account does not tell us what made Hobab join Moses. Was it a conviction from God that this was the right way forward? Pity or compassion for Moses? A puffed-up desire to be a hero? It could have been a combination, as we often have mixed reasons for undertaking new ventures. Even though our hearts may not be pure, God still uses us. He changes our sometimes divided hearts, cleansing them and making us whole.

When I am out walking in the park, often I am in my own world. One day, however, I heard another American accent. After walking past the speaker, I felt the nudge to talk to her, but I resisted. As I continued my circuit, the feeling remained. Finally, I did strike up a conversation after all and learned that the woman was newly transplanted and had been feeling lonely and disconnected. Our conversation brought her encouragement. On a much larger scale, Hobab changed his plans radically, saying yes to Moses. Moses was then able to follow God in the wilderness through the ark, complemented by Hobab's hands-on experience. A good partnership indeed.

Prayer

Lord, show me the places where I have dug in my heels. Soften my heart.

AMY BOUCHER PYE

RUTH 1:15–17 (NIV)

Your people, my people

> 'Look,' said Naomi, 'your sister-in-law is going back to her people and her gods. Go back with her.' But Ruth replied, 'Don't urge me to leave you or to turn back from you. Where you go I will go, and where you stay I will stay. Your people will be my people and your God my God. Where you die I will die, and there I will be buried. May the Lord deal with me, be it ever so severely, if even death separates you and me.'

About 15 years ago, a verse from the book of Ruth was impressed on my mind as my new husband and I approached the town where he would be a curate: 'Your people will be my people and your God my God'. The thought was daunting, for I had not long come to the UK and was still getting used to the ways of my new countrypeople. As we drove along the high street, these words continued to reverberate within me—so much so that I wondered if living there would entail a cost.

Our time there was cut short, for tensions within the parish meant that the vicar was signed off on stress-related sick leave. My husband was left adrift and I began to consider whether I really did want 'these people' to be 'my people', for I had witnessed behaviour that left me sad and disquieted. I knew, however, that, whatever their actions, these were still 'my people', for I, too, had the propensity for similarly uncharitable thoughts and deeds.

In the book of Ruth, we see a daughter-in-law so committed to her dead husband's mother that she is willing to forsake her country and move with Naomi back to Bethlehem. Ruth becomes a pilgrim, serving her mother-in-law with grace and selflessness. For many, the story is familiar—Naomi finds a relative who agrees to marry Ruth, thus redeeming her under the law so that she can carry on the family line. Ruth and Naomi's needs for protection, care and love are met.

All over the world, God's people are our people. Who will he send across your path today?

Prayer

Lord, open my eyes and my heart to embrace your children.

AMY BOUCHER PYE

Psalm 84:1–5 (NIV)

A joy and an ache

How lovely is your dwelling place, Lord Almighty! My soul yearns, even faints, for the courts of the Lord; my heart and my flesh cry out for the living God. Even the sparrow has found a home, and the swallow a nest for herself, where she may have her young—a place near your altar, Lord Almighty, my King and my God. Blessed are those who dwell in your house; they are ever praising you. Blessed are those whose strength is in you, whose hearts are set on pilgrimage.

As an American in the UK, some high days and holy days bring me not only joy but also a corresponding ache as I am far away from family and friends. I experience the most profound ache and longing on Thanksgiving, which this year falls tomorrow. I feel the loss of the feasting around a table heaped with turkey, stuffing and gravy and the friendship and lively conversation that ensue. Of course, I understand why Brits do not celebrate Thanksgiving: after all, the Pilgrims were giving thanks for escaping religious persecution in England! Such is the friendship between the countries now, that I attend a special Thanksgiving service at St Paul's Cathedral each year, yet the ache and longing remain.

Living today, I enjoy a mobility never imagined by the Pilgrims. My seven-hour plane ride is a blip compared with their five-month journey across the choppy Atlantic in 1620. After they survived their first harsh winter, they invited the Native Americans who had helped them acclimatise to join in a three-day feast of thanksgiving. Thus the tradition began, being formally added to the calendar when, in 1863, the then president Abraham Lincoln declared that there be a national day of Thanksgiving each November.

Our psalm today reflects the greater ache that all pilgrims feel—for sweet fellowship with God. Our experiences of love, community, belonging and celebration are rooted in his character and our longings for these experiences are a harbinger of what is to come when we are reunited with God in heaven.

Reflection

'He anointed us, set his seal of ownership on us, and put his Spirit in our hearts as a deposit, guaranteeing what is to come' (2 Corinthians 1:21–22).

Amy Boucher Pye

COLOSSIANS 2:6–7 (NIV)

Give thanks

So then, just as you received Christ Jesus as Lord, continue to live your lives in him, rooted and built up in him, strengthened in the faith as you were taught, and overflowing with thankfulness.

The Pilgrims, devout in their faith, left England in 1608 for Amsterdam in search of religious freedom. They lived there for twelve years before the foreign culture wore them down and they decided to head for the 'New World'. Their journey on the *Mayflower* was desperate. The ship was designed for carrying cargo, not passengers, and the cabin where they slept was intended for 30 people, not 80. Their food rotted and was infested with weevils; they nearly drowned when the ship's main beam cracked; they endured ridicule from the sailors.

When they finally arrived in the New World, the Pilgrims still faced challenges—building homes, growing food, caring for the sick and dying. In all things, however, they gave thanks and observed a full day of sabbath each week. They also decided to have a thanksgiving feast. During this three-day celebration, they gave thanks for their food, having built seven houses, a peace treaty with the Native Americans and, most importantly, the freedom to worship God. The women cooked, the men played games and they all shared stories and gave thanks.

This, then, is the heritage of Americans, who, for one holiday at least, eschew commercialism and come together at Thanksgiving to enjoy good food and each other's company. Many Christians keep up the tradition of sharing stories of thankfulness around the table. With the telling and the listening, they become strengthened in their faith, as we see in our passage from the apostle Paul's letter to the Colossians.

The challenges we face will differ from those of the Pilgrims, but we can follow their example of devotion to God, taking risks, reaching out to different people and taking time to celebrate and give thanks. We may not be eating turkey today, but we all can take a moment to 'give thanks to the Lord for he is good' (Psalm 107:1).

Reflection

'When he was at the table with them, he took bread, gave thanks, broke it and began to give it to them' (Luke 24:30).

AMY BOUCHER PYE

PSALM 39:12–13 (NIV)

The sin that separates

Hear my prayer, Lord, listen to my cry for help; do not be deaf to my weeping. I dwell with you as a foreigner, a stranger, as all my ancestors were. Look away from me, that I may enjoy life again before I depart and am no more.

This song, probably from King David, expresses repentance. Stricken with illness, David hates God's silence and pleads for the Lord to bridge the distance that has become a wedge between them. The silence makes him feel like a foreigner and a stranger from God. Bereft, he seeks the restoration of their relationship.

From the point of view of pilgrimage, this psalm echoes the theme of the dislocation pilgrims can feel. The Hebrew words that David uses for 'alien' and 'stranger' broaden our understanding of this sense of not being at home (see *The NIV Application Commentary: Psalms*). The Hebrew word for 'alien' (or foreigner) was used to refer to someone who was not an Israelite but inhabited the promised land, though without full rights. They may have been servants or employees of Israelite families, for example. Another meaning of the word is people not living in their native lands. Thus, this term could be applied to the Israelites themselves as they travelled to Canaan.

To be a stranger and a foreigner at that time meant living with tenuous rights. The landowner could become fickle and throw them out. Their ability to prosper was limited. That is how the psalmist feels—he knows that his sin has spoiled his standing as a favoured son. Now he is on the outside, looking in. He is as the prodigal son, tending the pigs and yearning for his father's embrace.

Because we are sinful, our journeys entail times of separation from God due to our wrongdoing, but, as with David and the prodigal son, when we repent, God, in his mercy, closes the gap. He runs towards us, embraces us, puts on the prized coat over our pig-slopped clothes and rejoices that we are home.

Reflection

'Let's have a feast and celebrate. For this son of mine was dead and is alive again; he was lost and is found' (Luke 15:23–24).

AMY BOUCHER PYE

JEREMIAH 50:4–5 (NIV)

True repentance

'In those days, at that time,' declares the Lord, 'the people of Israel and the people of Judah together will go in tears to seek the Lord their God. They will ask the way to Zion and turn their faces toward it. They will come and bind themselves to the Lord in an everlasting covenant that will not be forgotten.'

These few lines of prophecy about the Israelites come in the midst of a greater warning from the prophet Jeremiah to the people of Babylon. At that time, the Israelites had split into the northern and southern kingdoms and, thus, lived in a state of disunity. Jeremiah is known as the weeping prophet because his words from the Lord are often of impending destruction.

The prophecy here speaks of God's people who have turned away from him. No longer are they eager to follow his laws and decrees. A series of corrupt kings have added to the debauchery, but Jeremiah tells of a time when the people of both kingdoms will bow their knees and return to the Lord. With tears they will seek the way of Zion.

We might find the book of Jeremiah depressing, but verses such as these—tucked away in the midst of prophecies of doom—bring hope. Our pilgrimages are often filled with wrong or missed turnings, whether through sins of omission or commission. When we seek the Lord, however, he will extend to us his everlasting covenant.

The Lord does not demand that we come to him with weeping before he will forgive us, but tears of remorse are often a sign of true repentance. Sometimes when I am having to discipline my children, I see them move from being somewhat sorry for their actions to being deeply so—perhaps because of the consequences I have to convey to them. The humiliation of the naughty chair (or, worse, the pain of lost screen time) often brings about true sorrow for the infraction. What will it take for us to repent?

Prayer

'Have mercy on me, O God, according to your unfailing love; according to your great compassion blot out my transgressions. Wash away all my iniquity and cleanse me from my sin' (Psalm 51:1–2).

AMY BOUCHER PYE

LUKE 9:51–58 (NIV)

Set towards Jerusalem

As the time approached for him to be taken up to heaven, Jesus resolutely set out for Jerusalem. And he sent messengers on ahead, who went into a Samaritan village to get things ready for him; but the people there did not welcome him, because he was heading for Jerusalem. When the disciples James and John saw this, they asked, 'Lord, do you want us to call fire down from heaven to destroy them?' But Jesus turned and rebuked them. Then he and his disciples went to another village. As they were walking along the road, a man said to him, 'I will follow you wherever you go.' Jesus replied, 'Foxes have dens and birds have nests, but the Son of Man has no place to lay his head.'

At the start of our second week on the subject of pilgrimage, we turn to the life of Jesus. In one sense, his whole human life was a pilgrimage—namely as one of the Godhead who became man and dwelt among us before returning to heaven.

Today's reading comes as Jesus sets out for Jerusalem and the cross, knowing the sacrifice that he will make. As part of this, he begins preparing his disciples for his death. When James and John think that the unwelcoming village will need to be punished, Jesus rebukes them. Rather than punishment, this was a time for grace and proclamation.

Then another man appears, saying that he wants to follow Jesus—probably as one would follow a rabbi, learning from him by walking with him. Jesus replies that though even the wild animals have holes in which to escape, he does not enjoy such a refuge. The cost of following him will be great, but the rewards will be eternal.

We often shy away from speaking of the sacrifice required of disciples of Christ when sharing with someone enquiring about our faith. Jesus, in contrast, is clear. May he give us appealing words filled with the right balance of grace and truth.

Prayer

Lord God, sometimes we fear that you will make us renounce what we love. Give us strength and courage to follow you and put hope and faith in our hearts that we may believe your promises.

AMY BOUCHER PYE

MARK 10:28–30 (NIV)

Gifts now and later

Then Peter spoke up, 'We have left everything to follow you!' 'Truly I tell you,' Jesus replied, 'no one who has left home or brothers or sisters or mother or father or children or fields for me and the gospel will fail to receive a hundred times as much in this present age: homes, brothers, sisters, mothers, children and fields—along with persecutions—and in the age to come eternal life'.

Our text comes just after the rich man asks Jesus how he can enter the kingdom. Jesus' words to him are stark: sell his possessions, give to the poor and follow him. The disciples are amazed. Then Jesus gives the assurance above—those who renounce family members and livelihoods and who endure ill treatment for his sake will receive a hundredfold blessings.

This passage makes me think of missionaries of old, who would leave their homes for far-flung countries, never to return or else come back decades later to a few remaining relatives whom they might not recognise. James Fraser (1886–1938) was such a pilgrim. He gave up what would have been a budding career as an engineer—or a concert pianist—to live among the remote tribal people in China. What he relinquished was great, but what he gained was everlasting, for, through his dependence on God—as expressed through a disciplined programme of prayer (shared with his prayer partners at home)—he witnessed many Lisu Chinese people coming to faith.

God might not be asking us to be mission partners in a remote village, but what he seeks in us, as with the young rich man, is a heart willing to eschew the things that may have become idols to us—even our family members or our homes or our work. Can we say 'yes' to Jesus as he asks us to follow him, trusting that we will receive a hundred times what we are saying 'no' to?

Reflection

'Now to him who is able to do immeasurably more than all we ask or imagine, according to his power that is at work within us, to him be glory in the church and in Christ Jesus throughout all generations, for ever and ever!' (Ephesians 3:20–21).

AMY BOUCHER PYE

ROMANS 12:1–2 (NIV)

A perfect sacrifice

Therefore, I urge you, brothers and sisters, in view of God's mercy, to offer your bodies as a living sacrifice, holy and pleasing to God—this is your true and proper worship. Do not conform to the pattern of this world, but be transformed by the renewing of your mind. Then you will be able to test and approve what God's will is—his good, pleasing and perfect will.

The apostle Paul, in writing to the Romans, has, in the first eleven chapters, delivered a lot of theology—salvation, justification, righteousness, freedom. Then he pens a big 'therefore'. 'Listen up,' he seems to say. 'This is how to live it out.'

Today's reading concerns the internal transformations that take place in pilgrims, resulting in changes in behaviour. Paul tells the Romans to start by offering their bodies to God. No longer do they make animal sacrifices, for the new covenant brought forth by Jesus supersedes that. Rather, now they give themselves as living sacrifices and God will not reject them as he would previously an imperfect dove or bull.

Then Paul says not to conform. Living in a caustic world, we can easily sink to the level of the prevailing culture as we give in to gossip, angry thoughts and bitter recriminations, but God, through his indwelling Spirit, will change the pattern of our thoughts as we submit to him.

We may be familiar with the name of the 17th-century monk Brother Lawrence, for he coined the concept of practising the presence of God. While working in the monastery kitchen, he would call to mind—moment by moment—that God lived in his soul and body through the Spirit and Son. This humble monk was transformed. We, too, can practise this, perhaps by setting an hourly alarm on our mobile phones or doing so each time we cross the road or when we are about to blast out a series of unhelpful or hurtful words.

When we are transformed, then we will understand how God wants us to live. We will learn his 'good, pleasing and perfect will'.

Reflection

'So whether you eat or drink or whatever you do, do it all for the glory of God' (1 Corinthians 10:31).

AMY BOUCHER PYE

2 Corinthians 5:1–4 (NIV)

Our flimsy tent

For we know that if the earthly tent we live in is destroyed, we have a building from God, an eternal house in heaven, not built by human hands. Meanwhile we groan, longing to be clothed instead with our heavenly dwelling, because when we are clothed, we will not be found naked. For while we are in this tent, we groan and are burdened, because we do not wish to be unclothed but to be clothed instead with our heavenly dwelling, so that what is mortal may be swallowed up by life.

When I was growing up, I would go on a yearly wilderness canoe trip in northern Minnesota. We would eschew plumbing and comfortable beds for the wonders of being close to nature, with just a flimsy tent between us and the outside world. Most nights we would sleep well, if in somewhat cramped conditions, a cool breeze wafting through the screen, but one night stands out in my memory. The rains felt like a flood and our tent's walls became saturated with water. Droplet after droplet came in, soaking our sleeping bags and making us miserable. We wondered if the night would ever end.

Tents are flimsy things, but necessarily so, for who would want to haul bulky boards and nails on a long journey? So, too, are our bodies, as the apostle Paul says here in his letter to the Corinthians. Our culture resists Paul's words, with its ever more invasive forms of plastic surgery to stave off ageing. Alternatively, it offers the latest miracle cream to reduce wrinkles or the latest gadget, car or trophy partner. Paul, though, speaks of the eternal realities under which we live.

Our hope is in heaven, when we will enjoy a dwelling made with the best building materials, which will never leak, rot, get mouldy or break. We will not need Botox or surgery or hugely expensive face creams, Ferrari, yacht or smartphone. None of that will matter—it will be 'swallowed up'—as we embrace true living. Come, Lord Jesus!

Prayer

Lord, we want to not be overly concerned with our earthly tent. Help us to focus on what truly matters.

Amy Boucher Pye

Hebrews 11:8–10 (NIV)

Pilgrims by faith

By faith Abraham, when called to go to a place he would later receive as his inheritance, obeyed and went, even though he did not know where he was going. By faith he made his home in the promised land like a stranger in a foreign country; he lived in tents, as did Isaac and Jacob, who were heirs with him of the same promise. For he was looking forward to the city with foundations, whose architect and builder is God.

As we near the end of our journey, engaging with the concept of pilgrimage, we return to Abraham, Isaac and Jacob through a faith-building passage from the letter to the Hebrews. This chapter lists hero after hero in the Bible who followed God's call on their life. They lived by faith while enduring hardship and welcomed from afar the fulfilment of the promises of God.

For me, a line from our passage that stands out is that Abraham did not know where he was going. He did not have the latest GPS, his travel route planned out in detail down to which hotel he would stay in on night 23. Rather, he set out blind, trusting God with herds and servants and household goods, journeying on laboriously.

I am somebody who is directionally challenged, so the thought of going on a journey without Gertie (our name for our GPS) sends shivers down my spine. I am a much more content traveller when someone is navigating—at least when it is a physical journey.

Abraham made mistakes: to Pharaoh, he passed off his wife as his sister so that the Egyptians would not kill him; he gave in to Sarah's request that he sleep with her maid so as to hurry up the process of having the promised heir. Yet, the writer to the Hebrews does not mention these errors of judgment. Rather, he says simply that Abraham obeyed and went. I find that encouraging. Though we may follow the wrong course or go off-track, God forgives us and, if we are faithful, he will say of us that we, too, obeyed and went.

Prayer

Lord God, direct my footsteps this day, that I might walk the path that leads to joy, peace and righteousness.

Amy Boucher Pye

Friday 30 November

Hebrews 11:13–16 (NIV)

Aim at heaven

All these people were still living by faith when they died. They did not receive the things promised; they only saw them and welcomed them from a distance, admitting that they were foreigners and strangers on earth. People who say such things show that they are looking for a country of their own. If they had been thinking of the country they had left, they would have had opportunity to return. Instead, they were longing for a better country—a heavenly one. Therefore God is not ashamed to be called their God, for he has prepared a city for them.

One night, as we and our children were discussing the evening's Bible story—Jesus with the woman at the well—we were talking about nationalities, for Jesus, as a Jewish man talking with a Samaritan woman, would have broken social conventions. We discussed national allegiances, as our children have two: British and American. My son said that he felt more British than American—much to my chagrin.

The kids—and now I—have dual citizenship, but, as Christians, we all have dual or triple or more citizenship, with our most important passport aligning us to the heavenly country. We hold our earthly citizenship lightly, knowing that our lives here are a tiny dot compared with eternity.

These verses from Hebrews underline how the ancients were living in view of heaven. The passage forms an interlude, when the writer pauses in his great list of the heroes who lived by faith to emphasise their eternal perspective. As with the psalm we read last Friday that spoke of being a foreigner and stranger, the heroes listed in Hebrews also knew that their heavenly passport was the important one.

Are we living in the light of eternity? One way I like to get heaven into my imagination, so to speak, is to chew over the last chapters of Revelation. The imagery soaks into my heart and mind and, for a few minutes at least, the cares of this world lessen.

Reflection

Aim at heaven and you will get earth 'thrown in':
aim at earth and you get neither.

C.S. Lewis, *Mere Christianity* (1952)

Amy Boucher Pye

Saturday 1 December

Revelation 21:3–4 (NIV)

We will be his people

And I heard a loud voice from the throne saying, 'Look! God's dwelling place is now among the people, and he will dwell with them. They will be his people, and God himself will be with them and be their God. "He will wipe every tear from their eyes. There will be no more death" or mourning or crying or pain, for the old order of things has passed away.'

When I was in my 20s, I was at the bedside of my friend's brother when he died from a terminal illness. The mundane and the holy mixed and mingled for, as his breathing became laboured, one of us overturned a glass of fizzy drink. While those nearest cleaned up the spill, I realised that Richard's breaths were coming even farther apart. I motioned them over and we entered a holy moment as we witnessed him move from this life to the next. It felt like a window into another world. My friend said later how it was like giving birth—great pain, but great joy.

Although he died in his 40s, it was a good death. Only days before, we had gathered around his bed for his baptism. The room was pungent with the fragrance of tiger lilies and the scent of new life in the midst of earthly death. There was pain, but there was hope and rejoicing, too.

We also will reach the pinnacle of our pilgrimage when we are united with God in heaven. There we will no longer have laboured breaths or terminal illnesses or grieving siblings and friends. God himself will be with us, dwelling with us and making all things new. We will feel his embrace and hear his, 'Well done, my good and faithful servant.' No longer will we become weary or endure pain or suffer heartbreak. Instead, we will have joy—everlasting, abundant, overflowing joy.

Heaven will be the prize of a life lived well. May we dwell under its shadow this day.

Prayer

'The Spirit and the bride say, "Come!" And let him who hears say, "Come!" Whoever is thirsty, let him come; and whoever wishes, let him take the free gift of the water of life' (Revelation 22:17).

Amy Boucher Pye

Bible stories rediscovered: Joshua and the battle of Jericho

Joshua fighting the battle of Jericho—it is a real Sunday school favourite because it is so wonderfully dramatic. There is the curious liturgical marching, the unusual prescription of once a day for six days, then seven on the seventh day. It all builds to the climax, when the walls come down.

The way the story is told in the book of Joshua is, surprisingly, about two people. The first is Joshua. Moses first chose him as an assistant leader when he was a young man. He was one of the two spies who returned from the promised land with a positive report, based on his trust in God. Now, around 70 years old, he is finally entrusted with the leadership of the people of Israel. His mission is to take them over the Jordan, conquer Canaan and turn his vast tribe from desert nomads into pastoral agriculturalists.

God's message of preparation is highly appropriate—to us, as well as Joshua: 'Be strong and very courageous. Be careful to obey... Keep this Book of the Law always on your lips; meditate on it day and night, so that you may be careful to do everything written in it... do not be discouraged, for the Lord your God will be with you wherever you go.' (Joshua 1:7–9). How would he work this out faced with his first serious obstacle—the massive walls of Jericho?

Another person shares top billing in this drama. The contrast with Joshua could not be greater. Rahab is a woman, foreigner, prostitute, liar and traitor... and hero. She risks her life because she is convinced about God. She shelters the spies sent by Joshua, helps them escape and, when destruction comes, is rescued.

Jericho is a milestone in God's great story of salvation revealed through the people of Israel. He had brought them out of Egypt and led them through the wilderness to the promised land. Now there was an obstacle to be overcome. At this point, God reveals that, in the midst of destruction, he is ready and able to rescue the unlikeliest of people. Now that's encouraging.

Are you ready to cross the Jordan?

Stephen Rand

JOSHUA 1:1–5, 9 (TNIV, ABRIDGED)

Get ready: I will be with you

After the death of Moses the servant of the Lord, the Lord said to Joshua son of Nun, Moses' assistant: 'Moses my servant is dead. Now then, you and all these people, get ready to cross the River Jordan into the land I am about to give to them—to the Israelites. I will give you every place where you set your foot, as I promised Moses... As I was with Moses, so I will be with you; I will never leave you nor forsake you... Be strong and courageous. Do not be afraid; do not be discouraged, for the Lord your God will be with you wherever you go.'

It is Advent Sunday—time to start preparing for Christmas. Once again, the wonderful story of God's intervention in human history begins, but we are about to spend time with Joshua, not Jesus; to focus on a battle, not the Prince of Peace. What are the links between the two?

Let us start with their names. Jesus is the Greek form of Joshua. The two names, essentially, have the same meaning: Saviour: 'You are to give him the name Jesus, because he will save his people from their sins' (Matthew 1:21)

Moses had brought the people thus far to the promised land, but Joshua would lead them over the Jordan to claim their God-given inheritance. As Joshua completed the rescue begun by Moses, so Jesus came to fulfil the law given by Moses. The law could not bring forgiveness, salvation and life with God—but Jesus could and did... and still does.

'Joshua fought the battle of Jericho', as the song goes. Jesus, Prince of Peace, had to fight a battle. As Paul writes, we have 'peace through his blood shed on the cross' (Colossians 1:20). The great Victorian preacher Charles Spurgeon put it like this: 'No more doth Joshua lift sword or spear on behalf of Israel, but Jesus still rideth forth, conquering and to conquer, and all his people have victory through his blood.'

Reflection

As you prepare for Christmas, may you know Jesus' victory, presence and peace as you hear his voice saying, 'I will be with you.' Then you can be strong and very courageous.

STEPHEN RAND

JOSHUA 5:13–14 (TNIV)

With God on our side

Now when Joshua was near Jericho, he looked up and saw a man standing in front of him with a drawn sword in his hand. Joshua went up to him and asked, 'Are you for us or for our enemies?' 'Neither,' he replied, 'but as commander of the army of the Lord I have now come.' Then Joshua fell facedown to the ground in reverence.

Joshua is on the threshold of a major challenge. Jericho is a significant obstacle that must be overcome if he—and the people—are to move forward. At this moment, he has a strange encounter. He meets a man with a drawn sword who reacts like a sentry: 'Whose side are you on?'

The answer is surprising. Surely the commander of the Lord's army would be on the side of God's people, but that is not the case. Joshua is not given any promise of automatic support. God's power is not put into any human pocket. No individual or nation can ever assume that God is his or hers. The reverse is true—they are God's and he demands obedience.

I have been a massive fan of Bob Dylan ever since my early teens. That was when I first heard his bitter anti-war song about those who fought their earthly battles claiming they did so 'With God on our side'. He concluded that if God is on our side, 'he'll stop the next war'.

We are right to be wary of leaders and politicians who send armies into battle and slaughter thousands of human beings with the assertion that God is on their side. At the same time, we can be confident that, in our own spiritual battles, as we struggle to live God's way and do what is right, God is on our side. We can trust him to strengthen us, equip us and, ultimately, win the victory.

The baby who came at Christmas is indeed the commander of the army of the Lord, the Prince of Peace.

Prayer

Almighty God, help us to fight for what is right and for the rights of others. Help us to do all that makes for peace. Amen

STEPHEN RAND

JOSHUA 5:13–15 (TNIV, ABRIDGED)

Holy ground

Now when Joshua was near Jericho, he... saw a man standing in front of him with a drawn sword in his hand. Joshua... asked, 'Are you for us or for our enemies?' 'Neither,' he replied, 'but as commander of the army of the Lord I have now come.' Then Joshua fell face down to the ground in reverence, and asked him, 'What message does my Lord have for his servant?' The commander of the Lord's army replied, 'Take off your sandals, for the place where you are standing is holy.' And Joshua did so.

We take another look at this episode to see its outcome. What message was Joshua looking for? Perhaps he was looking for reassurance, a promise of victory or, perhaps, advice on battle tactics—after all, he was speaking to the commander of the Lord's army.

The message that came in answer to his request is as profound as it is unexpected. The whole enterprise of settling in the promised land was in the balance and Jericho was key to the process, but the message was not related to that immediate challenge. It is a reminder of a truth that underpins the history of the people of Israel. The place where they stood was holy—and was to be holy. It belonged to God. It was there for the service of God.

That is still true. God's presence makes the cathedral holy and it also makes the scrap-heap holy. There are no 'no go' areas for God. In the places where the spiritual battle is at its fiercest, we are still on holy ground.

Christians are bearers of God's presence. One day, years ago, I gave my Bible to Mother Teresa in Calcutta. She wrote in it, 'Be holy, because Jesus who loves you is holy.' Our calling as God's people is to carry the presence of Jesus, by his Spirit, everywhere we go and make it holy ground.

Advent is about the incarnation—and so are our lives.

Prayer

'O holy child of Bethlehem, be born in us today', so that our every step is on your holy ground. Help us remember that there is nowhere—and no one—not made holy by your presence.

STEPHEN RAND

JOSHUA 2:1, 9–11, 24 (TNIV, ABRIDGED)

A woman surrounded by fear

Then Joshua… secretly sent two spies from Shittim. 'Go, look over the land,' he said, 'especially Jericho.' So they went and entered the house of a prostitute named Rahab and stayed there… [She said], 'I know that the Lord has given this land to you… We have heard how the Lord dried up the water of the Red Sea for you when you came out of Egypt… When we heard of it, our hearts melted in fear and everyone's courage failed because of you, for the Lord your God is God in heaven above and on the earth below.'… [The two men…] said to Joshua, 'The Lord has surely given the whole land into our hands; all the people are melting in fear because of us.'

Joshua's encounter with Jericho began with a top-secret mission, which almost ended in disaster. The spies returned with the news that Jericho was full of fear—but only after they had been rescued by their 'landlady' Rahab. She is described as a 'prostitute'. It seems that in Jericho, then, as in so many parts of the world now, lodgings offered rather more services than were strictly necessary.

Rahab was no ordinary woman. When she realised who the men were, she decided to put her future in the hands of God. It cannot have been an easy decision. She was abandoning her heritage, her upbringing, her friends and family. She would have been seen as a traitor, but her leap of faith was based on evidence: she had heard what God had done and concluded that he must be the true God, the God of the whole earth.

Many women today from Islamic backgrounds are choosing to follow Jesus, risking everything because they are convinced that he is the one who offers life, even in the midst of fear. They take their places in the family of God. Rahab was written into the family tree that leads to the birth of Jesus (Matthew 1:5) and the brave women of the persecuted Church join all those who are 'born again' into the spiritual family whose head is Jesus.

Prayer

Father, send your Spirit now to strengthen all who choose to follow Jesus even when they are full of fear.

STEPHEN RAND

JOSHUA 6:1–5 (TNIV)

God's ways are not our ways

Now the gates of Jericho were securely barred because of the Israelites. No one went out and no one came in. Then the Lord said to Joshua, 'See, I have delivered Jericho into your hands, along with its king and its fighting men. March round the city once with all the armed men. Do this for six days. Make seven priests carry trumpets of rams' horns in front of the ark. On the seventh day, march round the city seven times, with the priests blowing the trumpets. When you hear them sound a long blast on the trumpets, make the whole army give a loud shout; then the wall of the city will collapse and the army will go up, everyone straight in.'

Jericho is surrounded, under siege. So, what next? Will it be slowly starved into surrendering? Attacked? Will there be a subterfuge to find a gap in its defences?

None of these. God's instructions are unique and slightly absurd: march round it for six days; on the seventh day, add a loud shout to the trumpet blast… and the walls will collapse. There must have been some raised eyebrows when Joshua told the others the plan!

Notice God's starting point. Before revealing any detail of the plan, there is an opening statement that is, in a sense, also a final statement: 'I have delivered Jericho into your hands.' It is not a promise: God did not say 'I will deliver…'. It has already been done: 'I have delivered…' The instructions, if followed, will reveal what is already a reality.

So it is for Christians. We already have eternal life. Our Saviour Jesus has delivered us from sin and death. We know the presence of God by his Spirit: one day we shall see him face-to-face.

Just as the people of Israel had to be obedient and march round Jericho for a week before they could see fully the reality that God has already secured, so we are called to live each day in the reality of what God has already done: 'as you have always obeyed… continue to work out your salvation with fear and trembling' (Philippians 2:12).

Reflection

Thank God that, as a Christian, you can live each day confident of Christ's ultimate victory.

STEPHEN RAND

Joshua 6:8–11 (TNIV)

Timing

When Joshua had spoken to the people, the seven priests carrying the seven trumpets before the Lord went forward, blowing their trumpets, and the ark of the Lord's covenant followed them. The armed guard marched ahead of the priests who blew the trumpets, and the rear guard followed the ark. All this time the trumpets were sounding. But Joshua had commanded the army, 'Do not give a war cry, do not raise your voices, do not say a word until the day I tell you to shout. Then shout!' So he had the ark of the Lord carried round the city, circling it once. Then the army returned to camp and spent the night there.

We have a slightly strange expression in English: 'the devil is in the detail.' It is strange because I think we could argue that God is in the detail as well! God gave Joshua his battle plan to pass on to the people. Now they are putting it into action, every detail—which means that, for six days, they have to do it silently. The trumpets will be blown, but, from the people, nothing. Then the moment will come—and it will be time to shout.

Timing is of the utmost importance: 'There is a time for everything, and a season for every activity under the heavens' (Ecclesiastes 3:1). I am sure that I need to know when to open my mouth and when to keep it shut! I recall that, many years ago, a friend insisted it was time to speak to another friend, to reveal that we knew of his immoral behaviour and it had to stop. I was not convinced that this was the right moment; years later the other friend was clear that the time was right and he was grateful for the intervention.

The older I become, the more I realise that discernment is perhaps the greatest spiritual gift of all. I have got my timing horribly wrong; sometimes I have got it right. Thank God he is in the detail. Thank God we can look to the Spirit for his guidance.

Prayer

Lord Jesus, help me to know when I should speak up
and when I should keep quiet.

Stephen Rand

JOSHUA 6:12–14 (TNIV)

Worship: the sound of the trumpet

Joshua got up early the next morning and the priests took up the ark of the Lord. The seven priests carrying the seven trumpets went forwards, marching before the ark of the Lord and blowing the trumpets. The armed men went ahead of them and the rear guard followed the ark of the Lord, while the trumpets kept sounding. So on the second day they marched around the city once and returned to the camp. They did this for six days.

I am very proud of my ram's horn trumpet. It accompanied me on my Jubilee Debt Campaign events. I once blew it outside the Treasury in London and the next day Gordon Brown announced that he was cancelling some significant debts of the world's poorest countries. There were some who thought I should have walked round the building seven times!

My trumpet fits in my inside jacket pocket. When I get the blowing right, it sounds quite impressive. I suspect the siege procession at Jericho featured the best, longest, loudest trumpets that the people possessed.

In the Bible, the trumpet represents the voice of God, announcing God's interventions in human history. The Jubilee trumpet was to be sounded in the fiftieth year, on the Day of Atonement, to proclaim liberty, announce a new start, debts being cancelled, the slate wiped clean (Leviticus 25:9–10). Also, the second Advent will be announced with a blast on the trumpet (1 Thessalonians 4:16).

The trumpet was used in worship and in battle and, at times in Israel's history, the two were clearly linked. As Christians, we are called into a spiritual battle—the battle for God's kingdom of justice and righteousness. Worship is an essential part of this battle. It is the opportunity to come together in the presence of the King of kings and, at its best, it stirs the heart and strengthens the soul. Perseverance and discipline are vital aspects of our life of worship. The people marched round Jericho the first day, the second day… and every day.

Prayer

Dear Lord, help me to worship you and live for you on the days when I do not feel like it. May my worship strengthen me for the battle. Amen

STEPHEN RAND

JOSHUA 6:15–16 (TNIV)

Victory!

> On the seventh day, they got up at daybreak and marched round the city seven times in the same manner, except that on that day they circled the city seven times. The seventh time round, when the priests sounded the trumpet blast, Joshua commanded the army, 'Shout! For the Lord has given you the city!'

Would you like to have been there? To add your voice to the shout of victory? It must have been a dramatic climax to the week of liturgical marching.

The people of Jericho had seen the procession every day. First, the honour guard, then the trumpet-blowing priests heralding the ark of the covenant—the symbol of the presence of God, then the long tail of the people winding their way round. Today, they kept going. Not once, not even twice, but seven times. Seven is a number that symbolises completeness and, on the seventh day, they walked round seven times: victory would be complete.

Note Joshua's command, that they were not to bring the walls down, but shout because God was giving them the city, as a shout of triumph, not a weapon of battle. This is a vital lesson to learn in our own lives. We are asked to be obedient, follow God's ways, but victory is not our doing—it is God's. He accepts us into his kingdom not because of what we have done, but because of what Jesus has done.

This is the essence of faith: we put our trust in someone else to achieve what we cannot achieve ourselves: 'God saved you by his grace when you believed. And you can't take credit for this; it is a gift from God. Salvation is not a reward for the good things we have done, so none of us can boast about it. For we are God's masterpiece. He has created us anew in Christ Jesus' (Ephesians 2:8–10, NLT).

God took the initiative for his people: he rescued them, led them, brought them to a new land, won a complete victory. It is the story of our salvation as he has done the same for us.

Reflection

'But thanks be to God! He gives us the victory through our Lord Jesus Christ' (1 Corinthians 15:57).

STEPHEN RAND

JOSHUA 6:17–19 (TNIV)

Devotion

[Joshua said] 'The city and all that is in it are to be devoted to the Lord. Only Rahab the prostitute and all who are with her in her house shall be spared, because she hid the spies we sent. But keep away from the devoted things, so that you will not bring about your own destruction by taking any of them. Otherwise you will make the camp of Israel liable to destruction and bring trouble on it. All the silver and gold and the articles of bronze and iron are sacred to the Lord and must go into his treasury.'

Yesterday, we noted that the victory came from God, not the people. It is at this moment that Joshua reminds them of the implications of how they behave after the battle. They are not to take any booty for themselves because they are not the victors—it does not belong to them. This was an extraordinary instruction in the light of the reality that is warfare down the ages, but God demanded discipline of his people. They were to set a different standard, not risk the pollution that would result from greed.

So, Jericho's wealth is reserved for God's treasury. This is its first mention in the Bible, but it will grow into the treasury that is part of the temple. Jesus watched a widow put her 'mite' into the same treasury and commended her for giving everything in terms of her meagre resources (Mark 12:41–44).

Giving is a vital part of Christian living. Sometimes we see it as giving God something that belongs to us, but the truth is, everything we have comes from God and he demands everything of us. Our giving of money to the church or to Christian organisations is part of the giving of ourselves, not a substitute for it.

There is also a difficult and awful reality in today's reading that cannot be glossed over and we will consider it tomorrow. Meanwhile, let us pray that churches will use the gifts entrusted to them to reflect God's love, generosity and compassion on the poor and the outcast.

Prayer

Generous God, allow me the joy of being open-handed rather than tight-fisted.

STEPHEN RAND

JOSHUA 6:20–21 (TNIV)

Destruction

When the trumpets sounded, the army shouted, and at the sound of the trumpet, when the men gave a loud shout, the wall collapsed; so everyone charged straight in, and they took the city. They devoted the city to the Lord and destroyed with the sword every living thing in it—men and women, young and old, cattle, sheep and donkeys.

The instruction was as clear as it was chilling: everything and everyone in Jericho (except Rahab and her household) was to be 'devoted' to God, which meant destroyed. The Hebrew word is *herem* and is sometimes translated 'cursed'. So, the moment of victory was followed by a genocide—an awful slaughter of every human being and animal.

The simplest—and undoubtedly overly simplistic—explanation is that the Canaanites, including the people of Jericho, were deeply contaminated by sin and evil, and sin, by its very nature, contaminates others. God had chosen the Israelites to be the people entrusted with bringing his saving grace to all of the world. If that was to be achieved, their distinctiveness needed to be protected.

This reality takes us to the edge of our understanding. Can this really be a God of love at work? The only answer I can hold on to is that this is a specific command for a specific situation—not a basis for any other group to decide it has a divine right to commit genocide—and it reveals an even deeper reality. The Bible is clear that sin has terrible and terrifying consequences. Children are abused, women trafficked, the poor exploited, families destroyed, communities torn apart. Ultimately, sin is the cause of death. It separates people from a holy and loving God. That is why, as God loved the world so much, he sent Jesus, born in a manger, to die for us so that the horrendous and eternal consequences of sin could be reversed. The awful judgment and justice of God are dealt with at the cross, where love and mercy meet.

Reflection

On the mount of crucifixion…
Grace and love, like mighty rivers, poured incessant from above
And Heav'n's peace and perfect justice kissed a guilty world in love.

William Edwards (trans.), *The Baptist Book of Praise*, 1900

STEPHEN RAND

JOSHUA 6:22–23 (TNIV)

The exception... and a promise kept

Joshua said to the two men who had spied out the land, 'Go into the prostitute's house and bring her out and all who belong to her, in accordance with your oath to her.' So the young men who had done the spying went in and brought out Rahab, her father and mother, her brothers and sisters and all who belonged to her. They brought out her entire family and put them in a place outside the camp of Israel.

There is a glimmer of hope. Joshua remembered the two spies had promised that Rahab would be spared in the slaughter. In the midst of the excitement and the awful turmoil, he ensured that the same two men, who would know best where to find her, were given the responsibility of keeping their promise.

Keeping promises is important. We make them and sometimes we break them, yet all know the pain of a broken promise if we are on the receiving end. It is one of God's essential characteristics that he keeps his promises. As Balaam explains to Balak: 'God is not a human, that he should lie, not a human being, that he should change his mind. Does he speak and then not act? Does he promise and not fulfil?' (Numbers 23:19). God's followers should be the same.

Rahab was relieved the two spies kept their promise and her rescue is given significant prominence within the story. It is as if the two realities of judgment and mercy are to be held in balance. Rahab is doubly unworthy of salvation: she is, in the eyes of the law of Israel, unclean by nature of her profession; she is also a member of the tribal group that has been identified for total destruction.

Yet, she is saved. Though this passage indicates that her 'uncleanness' prevented her from entering the camp of Israel, later we are told 'she lives among the Israelites to this day' (Joshua 6:25).

In the midst of judgment there is mercy; in the face of death there is life.

Reflection

Is there a promise you have made that you could keep today and bring blessing to one who needs to know somebody cares?

STEPHEN RAND

JOSHUA 6:27 (TNIV)

I'm a celebrity...

So the Lord was with Joshua, and his fame spread throughout the land...

The walls of Jericho came down... and Joshua's reputation increased dramatically. He was famous! Interestingly, the word translated 'fame' can also mean 'news'. Then, as now, if you made the news, you became famous. We now live in an age of celebrity. The media is full of news about celebrities, some of whom are only famous for being famous.

When young people are asked what they want to be when they grow up, they often reply, 'Famous.' One 13-year-old girl says, on the internet: 'I really badly want to be famous. It's my dream, I've had one dream in my life.' A newspaper reports that, in Spain, two teenage girls murdered a schoolfriend and told the judge they did it because they wanted to become famous. Joshua had not sought fame, though. He had been obedient to God and, as a result, had won a great victory.

I am a terrible namedropper. It has been my privilege to, occasionally, meet well-known people and I all too easily fall prey to the temptation to make the most of it: I have already done it in these notes! It has been an even greater privilege, however, to meet people who are not famous in the world's eyes, but who have achieved far more than any celebrity. How? Because they have lived lives informed and inspired by God's Spirit and seen individuals, families, whole communities transformed because, in the face of terror and persecution, they have trusted God and refused the easy, risk-free option.

When people live like that, they acknowledge that any recognition they might be given comes from the work of God's Spirit in their lives. John Wooden (1910–2010) was a Christian and a famous US basketball coach. He noted, 'Talent is God-given. Be humble. Fame is man-given. Be grateful. Conceit is self-given. Be careful.' Joshua reveals the right emphasis—the Lord was with him; everything else followed from that.

Reflection

John Wooden also said, 'Be more concerned with your character than your reputation, because your character is what you really are, while your reputation is merely what others think you are.'

STEPHEN RAND

JOSHUA 7:1, 20–21, 25 (TNIV, ABRIDGED)

Defeat in the jaws of victory

But the Israelites were unfaithful in regard to the devoted things; Achan... took some of them. So the Lord's anger burned against Israel... Achan replied [to Joshua], 'It is true! I have sinned against the Lord, the God of Israel. This is what I have done: when I saw in the plunder a beautiful robe from Babylonia, two hundred shekels of silver and a bar of gold weighing fifty shekels, I coveted them and took them. They are hidden in the ground inside my tent, with the silver underneath.'... Then all Israel stoned him.

What a tragedy! Just as Joshua's fame was spreading, the whole victory, marked by faith and obedience, was undermined by one man.

The story is a microcosm of human reality. First, the temptation came through sight: 'When I saw...' says Achan. We can be determined to do the right thing, but are so often betrayed by our eyes. I go to work determined to stick to my diet of healthy eating. The desk next to me is the one where the cakes are put so that everyone can share. I can see them... I cannot resist them. Sadly, temptation can be more serious. In 2 Samuel 11:2, only a few words are used to describe a life-and-death temptation: 'From the roof David saw a woman bathing. The woman was very beautiful...' Some 3000 years later, surveys suggest that over 50 per cent of Christian men, including pastors and leaders, struggle with internet pornography.

This leads us to the second truth: yielding to temptation is destructive. It cost Achan his life. Alcohol, drugs, sex—temptation that is not resisted is savagely destructive of individual lives. However large or small the temptation, it can lead to sin and sin is destructive.

Third, individual sins affect others. The whole of Israel suffered because of Achan's failure. Sin destroys relationships; marriages are broken, families shattered, churches compromised.

Churches must do more to help individuals resist temptation. Encourage small groups with genuine accountability, as it is when we are alone and think no one will know that we are most vulnerable.

Prayer

Lead us not into temptation, and deliver us from evil...

STEPHEN RAND

Saturday 15 December

HEBREWS 11:30–31; JAMES 2:24–26 (TNIV)

Saving faith

> By faith the walls of Jericho fell, after the army had marched round them for seven days. By faith the prostitute Rahab, because she welcomed the spies, was not killed with those who were disobedient... You see that people are justified by what they do and not by faith alone. In the same way, was not even Rahab the prostitute considered righteous for what she did when she gave lodging to the spies and sent them off in a different direction? As the body without the spirit is dead, so faith without deeds is dead.

People of faith are people who act on what they believe. The soldiers marched round Jericho because they believed what God said. They persevered. They kept going. The walls came down.

Across the world, walls are still coming down because people have faith in God and they keep on following God's plan, doing what is right—caring for the outcast, befriending the lonely, loving the unlovely, standing up for justice. You may be facing walls of your own: problems that seem insurmountable. Perhaps the story of Jericho will encourage you to keep going and know that you have enough faith to believe God is able to intervene and win the victory.

Then there is Rahab. She is a wonderful example of the truth that God is never ashamed of anyone who has faith in him—no one is outside the possibility of being part of his plan. While you may not identify with Rahab in any specific way, I know that there are many who are convinced they are not good enough, not qualified enough, not important enough for God.

Can you share the faith of Rahab and believe that you can be part of God's plans for his world and God will never be ashamed of you? In fact, he will write your name on the palm of his hand (Isaiah 49:16) for all the world to see. God is the one who specialises in making ordinary people special. That is why a baby—one of Rahab's descendants—was born in Bethlehem.

Prayer

Lord, grant me the faith that brings down walls and leads to actions bringing your life into every situation. Amen

STEPHEN RAND

2 and 3 John

When did you last receive a handwritten letter? For most of us, personal correspondence is a rare phenomenon these days. How delightful, then, to have not one, but two personal, profound and affectionate epistles before us this week.

Of all the New Testament correspondence, these are the most 'letter-like'. Each would have neatly filled a single, standard sheet of papyrus. One addresses a local church, the other an individual. Both summarise and apply the key themes of love and truth from the writer's earlier circular communication (1 John). Both conclude with the promise of a personal visit, with closing words so similar we shall only read them once.

'I have made this letter longer, because I have not had time to make it shorter', wrote philosopher Blaise Pascal (*Lettres Provinciales*, 1656–57). The apostle John could almost have said the opposite, for these brief documents contain the distillation of a lifetime's reflection on Jesus' teaching and apply it to specific and challenging situations.

John, the last surviving apostle, was at the close of his life when he set down what were probably the last portions of the Bible to be written. With the last living links to Jesus likely to be severed shortly and the canon of scripture yet to be formalised, the church was at a vulnerable stage in its history. Peripatetic teachers and prophets were an increasing and necessary part of the church scene. Most were sincere and devoted, but there were others who had realised that 'A clever rogue could make a comfortable living as a wandering prophet' (William Barclay, *The Letters of John and Jude*, 1971). Indeed, *The Didache*, the earliest 'instruction manual' for Christians, coined a word for such people: 'Christmongers'—those who traded in Christ. For them, 'prophet' equated to 'profit'. Emanating from John's pastoral heart, we sense in these letters a deep concern for vulnerable believers.

Lord Byron (1788–1824) wrote, 'One of the pleasures in reading old letters is the knowledge that they need no answer.' However, these ancient epistles do require a response. Their enjoinder to anchor our lives in truth and love, and their reminder of the Christian obligation to hospitality, resonate with all who seek to follow the way of Jesus.

Steve Aisthorpe

2 JOHN 1–4 (NIV)

Truth that transforms

> The elder, To the lady chosen by God and to her children, whom I love in the truth—and not I only, but also all who know the truth—because of the truth, which lives in us and will be with us for ever: Grace, mercy and peace from God the Father and from Jesus Christ, the Father's Son, will be with us in truth and love. It has given me great joy to find some of your children walking in the truth, just as the Father commanded us.

Considering how little ink was required to write this letter, it is incredible how much has been spent debating to whom it was addressed. Some suggest that it was written to a woman and her family, but most scholars see this as a letter to a church. So, Eugene Peterson begins his translation, 'My dear congregation' (*THE MESSAGE*). This understanding makes 'the children' members of that local Christian community. John had met some of them and was overjoyed to find them 'walking in the truth' (v. 4).

Truth is the dominant theme in John's opening remarks. He mentions it five times in four short verses. The truth (God's actions in history and their significance) can be 'known' (v. 1), but not in the way we might know cold facts. Rather, the truth is to 'live in us' (v. 2), changing us from the inside out.

As in many places throughout the UK, churches in my local city work together to train and mobilise teams of street pastors. These teams walk the city centre in the early hours, engaging with people, caring and listening. Recently, the project coordinator told me that the people they meet are generally less concerned with whether the claims of Christianity are true or not and more in whether 'it works'. They want to see truth lived out.

John challenges the contemporary notion that truth is a matter of opinion and he clearly expects that what we know should be reflected in how we live. Time and again, the actions of Jesus gave credibility to his words; over and over his words explained his actions.

Reflection

Jesus both proclaimed the truth and demonstrated that 'it works'.
He asks that we do likewise.

STEVE AISTHORPE

2 JOHN 5–6 (NIV)

The principal principle

And now, dear lady, I am not writing you a new command but one we have had from the beginning. I ask that we love one another. And this is love: that we walk in obedience to his commands. As you have heard from the beginning, his command is that you walk in love.

Whether a simple shack or a grand design, a building starts with its foundation. So John, a master builder of disciples and churches, before addressing a particular peril facing this church, checks the groundwork. There is nothing new here, only a reminder, but it is so crucial, so vital, that even in such a short note, he dare not exclude it. It is the most uncomplicated yet also the most demanding of commandments: 'love one another' (v. 5). Whatever challenges face a church, reinforcing this foundation is always the right starting point.

In his first letter, John made the astonishing declaration that 'God is love' (1 John 4:8). It reveals the very essence of God's character. In the light of this, it is unsurprising that 'God in flesh', Jesus Christ, and his first followers, should insist that love must be the hallmark and touchstone of his people (John 13:34; 1 John 3:23).

How can we grow in love? At times, Christ's expectations of his Church seem unattainable. Alone we cannot change, 'But the fruit of the Spirit is love' (Galatians 5:22). Archbishop William Temple illustrated it this way: 'It is no good giving me a play like *Hamlet* and telling me to write a play like that. Shakespeare could do it—I can't. And it is no good showing me a life like the life of Jesus and telling me to live a life like that. Jesus could do it—I can't. But if the genius of Shakespeare could come and live in me, then I could write plays like his. And if the Spirit of Christ could come into me, then I could live a life like His' (quoted in John Stott, *Basic Christianity*, 1958). God's love has been poured out into our hearts through the Holy Spirit (Romans 5:5).

Prayer

God of love, please cultivate more of your love in me. Amen

STEVE AISTHORPE

2 JOHN 7–11 (NIV)

True or false?

> Many deceivers, who do not acknowledge Jesus Christ as coming in the flesh, have gone out into the world. Any such person is the deceiver and the antichrist. Watch out that you do not lose what we have worked for, but that you may be rewarded fully. Anyone who runs ahead and does not continue in the teaching of Christ does not have God; whoever continues in the teaching has both the Father and the Son. If anyone comes to you and does not bring this teaching, do not take them into your house or welcome them. Anyone who welcomes them shares in their wicked work.

If you have a pound coin in your pocket, it could be worthless. According to the Royal Mint, there are 30 million fakes in circulation, but how are we to know if we have one of them? As with anything else that attracts the attentions of forgers, the starting point for spotting the counterfeit is always an intimate familiarity with the genuine.

John feared for the infant churches under his pastoral charge. Young believers were susceptible in ways never seen before or since. The remaining eyewitnesses to Jesus' earthly ministry were few. With the Bible yet to be compiled and codified, the scriptures in circulation were like the coins in our pockets—a mixture of bona fide and bogus.

Desperate times require desperate measures, but surely the same apostle who has been exhorting us to love one another cannot now be insisting on such fierce intolerance? Did not Jesus himself make it clear that the wheat and the weeds must be allowed to grow up side by side (Matthew 13:24–30)? Surely ours is not to judge?

John is not commending small-minded intolerance of anyone with values and beliefs contrary to our own. Any growing church will have its share of heresy! We each have to 'grow up' in faith (Ephesians 4:15), which inevitably means that a vibrant Christian fellowship will include people at various stages of development. John, however, refers here to 'deceivers': teachers who deny the basic truths of the gospel, especially the identity of Jesus Christ as the Word made flesh (John 1:14).

Reflection

As we become more acquainted with the genuine, the fake will be revealed.

STEVE AISTHORPE

3 John 1–4 (NIV)

Walk the talk

The elder, To my dear friend Gaius, whom I love in the truth. Dear friend, I pray that you may enjoy good health and that all may go well with you, even as your soul is getting along well. It gave me great joy when some believers came and testified to your faithfulness to the truth, telling how you continue to walk in it. I have no greater joy than to hear that my children are walking in the truth.

During the last decade, Jack was the most popular name for baby boys in England, every single year. The evidence we have from the first century shows that Gaius was the Roman equivalent. We should not assume, therefore, that the addressee of John's letter was any of the other men of that name we find elsewhere in the New Testament. Gaius' name was well chosen, however, as its root is the word for 'happiness' and, as news of Gaius reached John through the Christian grapevine, it filled him with 'great joy' (v. 3).

John's joy stemmed from hearing eyewitness reports that the transforming power of the 'Spirit of truth' (a common term for the Holy Spirit in John's Gospel and letters) was bearing fruit in the life of his 'dear friend' (vv. 1, 2, 11). Of course, John's sources had not literally seen the invisible, inner makeover that was going on, but they knew that his soul was 'getting along well' (v. 2) because they could observe its outworking. Gaius is reported to 'walk in the truth' (v. 4). In the New Testament, the term 'walking' is often used for the practical living out of faith.

Gaius had evidently allowed Christian truth to shape his character and direct his actions. He epitomised the term 'integrity', which literally means 'undivided'. The faith he professed and the lifestyle he practised were in harmony; there was no discord between belief and behaviour. No doubt his unified and wholehearted life not only brought joy to the apostle but was also a compelling witness to the not-yet-Christian people of his community and an inspiration to fellow believers.

Prayer

Lord, please grow more of your character in me—and may all I think, do and say reflect that inner change. Amen

Steve Aisthorpe

3 John 5–8 (NIV)

The love of strangers

> Dear friend, you are faithful in what you are doing for the brothers and sisters, even though they are strangers to you. They have told the church about your love. You will do well to send them on their way in a manner that honours God. It was for the sake of the Name that they went out, receiving no help from the pagans. We ought therefore to show hospitality to such people so that we may work together for the truth.

The term 'hospitality industry' says it all. In our own culture we have largely professionalised hospitality—trained staff extend a welcome for a price and guests expect nothing less than the service they pay for.

When John was writing, however, hospitality was a sacred duty as itinerant teachers were a crucial part of the fledgling church. A minority were frauds and John was adamant that there should be no welcome for them (2 John 7–11), but, while John was eager for the believers to avoid being hoodwinked by freeloaders, he longed for them to embrace the considerable blessings of genuine hospitality.

The word 'hospitality' in today's passage literally means 'love of strangers'. The New Testament reserves some of its warmest commendation for those who were exemplary in their hospitality—and some of its sternest condemnation for those who refused to be 'lovers of strangers'. Christian leaders are to be lovers of hospitality (Titus 1:8). Followers of Jesus Christ are to 'be eager to practise hospitality' (Romans 12:13, NLT). The earliest commentary on Romans captured the proactive sense of it perfectly and is a prophetic word to a culture that has institutionalised hospitality and encouraged fear of strangers: 'We are not just to receive the stranger when he comes to us, but actually to enquire often, look carefully for, strangers, to pursue them and search them out' (Origen, c.185–c.254).

John received accounts of Gaius' lifestyle and could tell that he was walking in the truth because his open heart had led to an open home and an open hand (vv. 5–8).

Reflection

'Do not forget to entertain strangers, for by so doing some people have entertained angels without knowing it' (Hebrews 13:2).

Steve Aishorpe

3 JOHN 9–11 (NIV)

Diotrephes: an example to avoid

I wrote to the church, but Diotrephes, who loves to be first, will not welcome us. So when I come, I will call attention to what he is doing, spreading malicious nonsense about us. Not satisfied with that, he even refuses to welcome other believers. He also stops those who want to do so and puts them out of the church. Dear friend, do not imitate what is evil but what is good. Anyone who does what is good is from God. Anyone who does what is evil has not seen God.

As I write these notes, bosses are getting a bad press. The latest film release is *Horrible Bosses*, the story of three friends who take revenge on their overbearing bosses. Today's newspapers carry details of research showing that senior managers are four times more likely to have psychopathic tendencies than the general population. It seems that Lord Acton's oft-quoted observation that 'power tends to corrupt and absolute power corrupts absolutely' (1887) does indeed have a basis in truth.

Diotrephes' rejection of legitimate authority (v. 9), his malicious gossip and determination that others should follow his unloving example (v. 10) all stem from a desire 'to be first' (v. 9). It is no secret that pride and vanity lie at the root of most conflicts in local churches.

John would remember his own quest for power, the indignant response of his fellow disciples and the gentle rebuke of Jesus as he explained the radically alternative dynamics of leadership in his upside down kingdom (Mark 10:35–45). He had no intention, however, of allowing the Diotrephes situation to fester. As we shall see tomorrow, rather than hide behind pen and ink, he plans to tackle the matter face to face in the near future (3 John:13–14). Despite being unrestrained in his unmasking of Diotrephes, he refused to enter into an arm's length war of words.

We all face the temptation to denigrate others for the sake of self-aggrandisement. It need not be blatant—just a subtle putting down, or a slight exaggeration in our own favour. Jesus, who 'did not come to be served, but to serve' (Matthew 20:28), leads us into another way.

Prayer

Jesus Christ, may you have supremacy in my life and your Church. Amen

STEVE AISTHORPE

3 JOHN 12–14 (NIV)

Demetrius: an example to follow

Demetrius is well spoken of by everyone—and even by the truth itself. We also speak well of him, and you know that our testimony is true. I have much to write you, but I do not want to do so with pen and ink. I hope to see you soon, and we will talk face to face. Peace to you. The friends here send their greetings. Greet the friends there by name.

During a 'quiet day', the retreat leader set me the task of prayerfully reviewing my life and expressing it as a 'map', noting the major junctions and what had happened there to take me in one direction rather than another. As I reviewed the map that emerged, I noted that, at each crossroads, there had been a significant person. In some cases, they were people with whom I had an ongoing relationship. In other cases, it seemed that God had brought them across my path for a particular reason or even at a specific moment.

Occasionally, such people challenged or even rebuked me. Often they encouraged me. On the whole, though, their influence was unconscious on their part. They each inspired me or confronted me not in their words but in their character, life and example. 'Mentors' have become fashionable in many contexts. The media expects high-profile personalities to be 'role models'. Sadly, a recent survey found that young people frequently choose role models from celebrity culture. We all need role models, but must choose them wisely.

Demetrius was an outstanding role model. Not only did John appreciate him but he was also 'well spoken of by everyone' and endorsed by the 'truth itself' (v. 12). The presence of Christ in his life was self-evident. Here was a man to learn from and be inspired by, someone with qualities to emulate. Jesus alone should be the ultimate focus of our attention (Hebrews 12:2) and the only yardstick for comparison (Ephesians 4:13). In his providence, however, God provides both role models and, amazingly and usually without our awareness, uses us to inspire, encourage and challenge others.

Reflection

Loving Father, thank you for each person you have used, and are using, to direct my path and shape my character. Amen

STEVE AISTHORPE

Christmas at the manger

In the weeks before Christmas, many homes and churches get out their nativity sets, which come in all shapes and sizes. Some may have painted figurines imported from Eastern Europe or elsewhere, others may be carved from olive wood from the Holy Land. Alternatively, they may be knitted, sewn or even made from Lego; they may be made of origami or come in the form of a children's pop-up book. They all, however, have more or less the same features: the holy family of Mary, Joseph and baby Jesus, some shepherds and lambs, a star and some angels, plus three Magi bearing their gifts. Some come complete with a stable, a few animals and an innkeeper, while some have a crib that is left empty until late on Christmas Eve, when the baby is finally added to complete the tableau.

It is a scene that is replicated in Christmas carols, school nativity plays and carol services. Anyone who reads the Bible carefully knows that the crib scene condenses events that occurred over many months, probably in several different places. Some of the figures that seem indispensible in the traditional crib scene are barely referenced in the Bible; some of the historical details of the story are disputed; some of the events are described in such strangely supernatural terms that it is hard to pick our way between metaphor and fact. Religious tradition, however, sometimes needs to let poetic licence override historical precision. The human race has been telling its salvation stories at least as far back as Abraham and, while those stories would not survive without a backbone of historical veracity, their function is not purely to preserve a historical record but also to reflect the evolving story of a faith that is passed on down the centuries, finding new resonances in every generation.

Over the coming days, let us look at the nativity figures, delve into the cracks between sentimentality and dry historical analysis and see if we can find some of the gems of truth in these ancient stories to illuminate our own lives. Due to the order of events in the stories—and the dates allocated in this issue of *New Daylight*—the description of Jesus' birth here falls on 28 December.

Maggi Dawn

LUKE 1:26–31 (NRSV)

Gabriel

In the sixth month the angel Gabriel was sent by God to a town in Galilee called Nazareth, to a virgin engaged to a man whose name was Joseph, of the house of David. The virgin's name was Mary. And he came to her and said, 'Greetings, favoured one! The Lord is with you.' But she was much perplexed by his words and pondered what sort of greeting this might be. The angel said to her, 'Do not be afraid, Mary, for you have found favour with God. And now, you will conceive in your womb and bear a son, and you will name him Jesus.'

It stands to reason that the annunciation must have happened months before Jesus' birth, but most school nativity plays still begin with the angel Gabriel visiting Mary. Blond curls and a white costume seem to be the top requirements for playing the part, to which are usually added a halo and some wings. Wings have a long history in our depictions of Gabriel—walk through an art gallery and you will see a winged angel in most annunciations. Intriguingly, though, Luke gives us no hint as to what Gabriel looked like, while other biblical accounts suggest that though the seraphim had wings, this messenger angel did not. The sixth-century Armenian gospel relates that Gabriel was invisible when he first greeted Mary. She prayed to God, thinking that the devil was tricking her. Only then did Gabriel materialise and announce his message clearly—and there is nothing to suggest that his appearance was anything other than human.

In the retelling of this story, with full awareness of its immense significance, layers of glitter and glory have accrued around this scene, but it is quite possible that Mary's experience was far subtler than our nativity plays suggest—perhaps much more like our own experience of prayer. In his poem 'Magnificat', Australian poet Noel Rowe says that the angel 'did not draw attention to himself', but came in quietly. Most of the time, that is how God speaks to us—not in the miraculous grandeur of a crib scene, but quietly, invisibly and in unremarkable ways.

Prayer

When you speak, God, help me to listen; help me to hear.

MAGGI DAWN

LUKE 1:34–35, 38 (NRSV)

Mary

> Mary said to the angel, 'How can this be, since I am a virgin?' The angel said to her, 'The Holy Spirit will come upon you, and the power of the Most High will overshadow you; therefore the child to be born will be holy; he will be called Son of God...' Then Mary said, 'Here am I, the servant of the Lord; let it be with me according to your word.' Then the angel departed from her.

Reading this passage, it is easy to assume that Mary replied to Gabriel instantly, without much need for thought. Other accounts, however, such as the Armenian gospel we considered yesterday and various poems and works of art, suggest a longer conversation. Edwin Muir, in his poem 'Annunciation', pictures Mary and the angel not just in a few moments of conversation, but as two creatures from different dimensions, entranced with one another 'through the endless afternoon' and locked in a silent, wondering gaze. Muir opens up the idea that Mary had time to consider the momentous message she had heard and then make her choice.

Wait—a choice? Was it not written in God's plan that Mary should bear Jesus? How could she have a choice? Theologians have pondered before now whether or not in fact there had been other 'Marys' before her who had said no. Mary is often painted as a mere girl, not someone who could think for herself or stand up to an angel, yet she did question Gabriel before acquiescing and it is equally possible that she could have rejected the call.

If we give too much weight to the idea that God has a plan, worked out in detail since time immemorial, then not only do we create a problem for holding religious truth in balance with scientific discovery but we also do damage to the theological truth that we are made in God's image—with free will and creative ability.

Vocation is never forced on anyone, whether male or female, powerful or seemingly insignificant. We are called to take part in God's work in the unfolding of creation and the story of salvation, but what we say 'yes' to is still up to us. We shape our own lives in conversation with God; we are not forced into a mould.

Prayer

God, please help me find my own voice as I listen to yours.

MAGGI DAWN

MATTHEW 1:18–20, 24 (NRSV)

Joseph

Now the birth of Jesus the Messiah took place in this way. When his mother Mary had been engaged to Joseph, but before they lived together, she was found to be with child from the Holy Spirit. Her husband Joseph, being a righteous man and unwilling to expose her to public disgrace, planned to dismiss her quietly. But just when he had resolved to do this, an angel of the Lord appeared to him in a dream and said, 'Joseph, son of David, do not be afraid to take Mary as your wife, for the child conceived in her is from the Holy Spirit…' When Joseph awoke from sleep, he did as the angel of the Lord commanded him; he took her as his wife.

Only rarely do we catch a glimpse of the subplots and secondary figures in the biblical narratives of Jesus' birth. Luke's Gospel only mentions Joseph in passing and even Matthew makes him seem like an accessory to the tale. Although Joseph is largely a background figure, these few verses show his part in the story to be vitally important.

Joseph was a practical man. He cared for Mary and kept her feet on the ground. He made sure she got out of Nazareth and came safely to Bethlehem. He may not have actually seen angels or been very visible in the story, but, without him, Mary could not have fulfilled her vocation and Jesus might not have survived into adulthood. Vocation, then, is not quite as much an individual issue as we sometimes like to think. Even though some get more of the limelight than others, it takes whole families, whole communities, to bring about the work of God.

Partners, parents or children of those with a strong sense of vocation might well look to Joseph for inspiration. Like him, they have lives of their own and it is calling enough simply to fulfil one's gifts to the glory of God and the benefit of the world. We also, however, have an important part to play in the vocations of those we love.

Prayer

We pray, God, that you would help us to discern our calling
and the callings of the people we love.

MAGGI DAWN

LUKE 2:1–5 (NRSV)

The donkey

In those days a decree went out from Emperor Augustus that all the world should be registered. This was the first registration and was taken while Quirinius was governor of Syria. All went to their own towns to be registered. Joseph also went from the town of Nazareth in Galilee to Judea, to the city of David called Bethlehem, because he was descended from the house and family of David. He went to be registered with Mary, to whom he was engaged and who was expecting a child.

Nativity scenes always depict Mary riding on a donkey. In fact, no donkey is mentioned in the Gospels, but, reading between the lines, it is assumed that there must have been one to make this journey possible and, over time, this beast of burden has become firmly and affectionately established in our annual retellings of the story.

Donkeys of various kinds do appear in other parts of the Bible. The story of Balaam's ass is a comical episode that has God giving speech to a 'dumb animal' to make a point to a reluctant prophet (Numbers 22:22–30). Another donkey carried Jesus into Jerusalem on Palm Sunday (Matthew 21:1–11) and the markings on donkeys' backs, which resemble a cross, add poignant symbolism to an everyday choice of transport.

The donkey, then, despite being absent from the biblical nativity stories, has taken on a certain significance in the crib scenes we see at Christmas. First of all, the donkey epitomises the way in which a 'dumb animal' might become the carrier of Christ and, as such, reflects the upside-down nature of the gospel, in which God has 'filled the hungry with good things, and sent the rich empty away' (Luke 1:53).

Second—and this aspect comes to life when animals are brought in to church or school nativity plays—they upset any notion that the gospel is limited to pristine beauty. There are plenty of jewel-encrusted, fabulous riches if you read through to the end of Revelation. While the gospel may end in a vision of spectacular beauty, it begins in the earthy and untidy smell and mess of life.

Prayer

Thank you, God, that your love and care extends to every part of life,
the earthly as well as the heavenly.

MAGGI DAWN

Luke 2:8–12 (NRSV)

The shepherds

In that region there were shepherds living in the fields, keeping watch over their flock by night. Then an angel of the Lord stood before them, and the glory of the Lord shone around them, and they were terrified. But the angel said to them, 'Do not be afraid; for see—I am bringing you good news of great joy for all the people: to you is born this day in the city of David a Saviour, who is the Messiah, the Lord. This will be a sign for you: you will find a child wrapped in bands of cloth and lying in a manger.'

Most first-century shepherds did not own their flocks, but worked as hired hands. They were the powerless and the voiceless; they lacked connections and qualifications and worked long, antisocial hours in tough conditions for very little pay. How refreshingly typical of the gospel, then, to reverse all expectations so that the shepherds were the very first to hear the news of Jesus' birth!

Professor Henri Nouwen experienced this kind of reversal when he left an academic career to work with profoundly disabled people in the L'Arche communities. He thought, at first, that he might have something to give to them, but, gradually, he came to believe he was receiving more than he was giving, for he discovered that the most fundamental level of human understanding is not intellectual, but instinctive. Education may help us to see some things more clearly—that is, surely, the point of it—but it does not qualify anyone for a front-row seat when it comes to the revelation of God. The mind is not superior to the heart when it comes to understanding what really matters.

Maybe it was precisely because the shepherds were not hampered by the need to reason and cross-reference what they heard that they had no trouble at all seeing the heavenly host in the sky above them, while the wise and educated missed it completely.

Prayer

God of love, tune us in to the voices of those who are often ignored and help us to respect, listen to and learn from the powerless.

Maggi Dawn

LUKE 2:17–20 (NRSV)

Mary ponders

When [the shepherds] saw this, they made known what had been told them about this child; and all who heard it were amazed at what the shepherds told them. But Mary treasured all these words and pondered them in her heart. The shepherds returned, glorifying and praising God for all they had heard and seen, as it had been told them.

When the shepherds saw Jesus, the vision of the heavenly host still fresh in their minds, they could not stop talking about what they had seen, but Mary stayed quiet and 'treasured all these words and pondered them'. This mirrors her response to Gabriel (1:34), where she also took time to absorb what she heard.

Even today, women may often be silent while men do most of the talking, but that does not mean they do not know what is going on. More significant, perhaps, is the hint that Mary only gradually came to understand the importance of the events she was caught up in. When we read the Gospel accounts of the nativity, it is easy to forget that they were written retrospectively, not merely recording events but explaining their meaning. Put yourself in Mary's shoes: this account of the shepherds' experience on the hillside is added to her curious encounter with the angel and her discussions with Elizabeth (Luke 1:39–56). She has not yet heard the words of Simeon (2:29–32) and Anna (v. 38) and does not know how things will play out. So, Mary ponders.

The word 'ponder' comes from Middle English, from the same root as the word for a 'pound' in weight. To ponder, then, is to weigh up events or information, consider their veracity and anticipate their consequences. The journey of faith is rarely revealed to us in advance, but is a matter of contemplating and considering what we learn as we go along. To echo something of the psalmist's words (131:1), I do not seek what cannot be known or fret over mysteries. The bigger part of spirituality is knowing that we do not know everything and being willing to live with shades of ambiguity and mystery.

Prayer

God of mystery, help me to live patiently when I do not understand.

MAGGI DAWN

MATTHEW 2:1–2, 7–10 (NRSV)

The star

In the time of King Herod, after Jesus was born in Bethlehem of Judea, wise men from the East came to Jerusalem, asking, 'Where is the child who has been born king of the Jews? For we observed his star at its rising, and have come to pay him homage.'... Then Herod secretly called for the wise men and learned from them the exact time when the star had appeared. Then he sent them to Bethlehem, saying, 'Go and search diligently for the child; and when you have found him, bring me word so that I may also go and pay him homage.' When they had heard the king, they set out; and there, ahead of them, went the star that they had seen at its rising, until it stopped over the place where the child was. When they saw that the star had stopped, they were overwhelmed with joy.

Few people take astrological charts seriously—particularly not the ones written for entertainment and so vague that anyone could read their 'fortune' into them. The kind of star-following that the Magi were engaged in was not mere superstition, but the cutting-edge science of first-century Persia. These highly educated men knew more chemistry, physics and cosmology than anyone else of their time. So, when they saw something extraordinary in the constellations, they were not merely following signs, but also absorbed in solving a scientific mystery so compelling that it took them through miles of inhospitable desert.

The shepherds had miraculous signs, but the journey the Magi made to the crib depended on their professional skills. Every twist in the tale was a puzzle without an answer, a sifting of incomplete information, a testing of hypotheses.

The star can remind us that most of us work out our faith through 'ordinary' means—reading, thinking and living our daily lives, rather than following a supernatural revelation. Faith is just as much a journey of reason as it is of experience—hard-won, puzzled-over and grasped only in tiny increments. Education and knowledge, then, are in no way to be feared; they can lead us to the very doorstep of heaven.

Prayer

Omniscient God, may we never be afraid that learning will pull us away from faith.

MAGGI DAWN

ISAIAH 9:2–6 (NRSV)

The empty crib

The people who walked in darkness have seen a great light; those who lived in a land of deep darkness—on them light has shined. You have multiplied the nation, you have increased its joy; they rejoice before you as with joy at the harvest, as people exult when dividing plunder. For the yoke of their burden, and the bar across their shoulders, the rod of their oppressor, you have broken as on the day of Midian. For all the boots of the tramping warriors and all the garments rolled in blood shall be burned as fuel for the fire. For a child has been born for us, a son given to us; authority rests upon his shoulders; and he is named Wonderful Counsellor, Mighty God, Everlasting Father, Prince of Peace.

As noted earlier, many nativity sets have a crib that is left empty until late on Christmas Eve, when the baby is added to complete the scene. Like Advent candles and calendars, this adds to the anticipation, but a religious scene with an absent Jesus is also a metaphor for those moments in life when it feels as if God has forgotten us.

Isaiah 9 is often read at Christmas, although verse 5 is sometimes left out, perhaps because 'boots of the tramping warriors' and 'garments rolled in blood' are thought unsuitable for children. It is worth remembering, however, that the story of salvation has always been told in the context of a deep emptiness and yearning. Such emptiness and yearning didn't end with Jesus, for, although he is the hub of the story, salvation is not yet complete. Paul's description of the Spirit as a 'down-payment' (2 Corinthians 5:5) is both a promise of better things to come and an acknowledgment that much of life is more like Advent or Lent than Christmas. When we are overwhelmed by our own trouble, or by the suffering of the world, we may sometimes wonder if there is any substance to faith. The empty crib reminds us that this ache for a better world is normal. God may seem to have vanished, but the promise still stands.

Prayer

God, when you seem to disappear, help me to remember your promise.

MAGGI DAWN

Monday 31 December

MATTHEW 2:12–1A (NRSV)

The end of the story...

Having been warned in a dream not to return to Herod, [the Magi] left for their own country by another road. Now after they had left, an angel of the Lord appeared to Joseph in a dream and said, 'Get up, take the child and his mother, and flee to Egypt, and remain there until I tell you; for Herod is about to search for the child, to destroy him.' Then Joseph got up, took the child and his mother by night, and went to Egypt, and remained there until the death of Herod.

The nativity scene ends with the holy family fleeing to Egypt in fear for their lives (v. 14) and the Magi taking a different route home. Pope Gregory the Great (c.540–604) gave a spiritual interpretation of the Magi's action, suggesting that, like them, having encountered Jesus, we are offered the chance, through repentance, to change the course of our lives. What about some of the other figures who featured in the story—the shepherds, for instance? They simply vanish into the background and, presumably, their lives returned to normal. We may wonder what they made of it all a year later.

After Christmas, when the feasting and celebrating is over, we take down the decorations, put our crib scenes away and return to our normal routines. What do we do when the Christmas story is over for another year?

For some people in some parts of the world, a dramatic change of heart or a religious experience may actually put them in some kind of immediate physical danger, and, like the holy family or the Magi, they may have to go into exile or hiding. For most of us, any transformation may seem undramatic on the surface. The inward change and the outworking of our salvation also affects everything, yet it is played out on the stage of everyday life. Let us pray that, like the shepherds, we will find the grace to continue to live out our faith in ordinary ways and places.

Prayer

Loving God, we pray for those who live under threat of religious persecution, and all who are simply working out their faith day by day.

MAGGI DAWN

The BRF

Magazine

Order Forms

The Managing Editor writes...

The BRF Magazine in this issue focuses mainly on the Advent and Christmas seasons, with contributions from Messy Church team member Jane Leadbetter, Barnabas Children's Ministry team member Martyn Payne and regular *New Daylight* contributor Rachel Boulding.

Martyn reminds us of the importance of listening hard to God for his leading, and Rachel, in the featured extract from her Advent book, also mentions the 'attitude of listening' and explains that we can only catch glimpses of the complexity of God's love for us.

During Advent, we prepare for the coming of Emmanuel, 'God with us'—yet it seems that we still need to search him out for ourselves, looking and listening carefully for signs of his presence. After all, the shepherds and the magi had to go looking for the child, even though they were told of his coming in remarkable ways.

We probably know the Christmas story very well, but many others in our society do not. Children need to hear it afresh—and Martyn Payne encourages us to celebrate the work of the Barnabas Children's Ministry team, who bring the Christian faith to life in schools up and down the country. Christmas shoppers in our town centres may know very little of the true meaning of the season—and Jane Leadbetter's innovative 'sheep trail' sends them off on a search for hidden signs of Jesus' coming among us. So those who do not yet participate in the Christian faith are given ways of seeing and hearing of God's love to us at Christmas time.

The old carol by Phillips Brooks, 'O little town of Bethlehem', says:

How silently, how silently
the wondrous gift is given.
So God imparts to human hearts
the blessings of his heaven.

We hope that BRF can offer ways for you to explore that quiet and wondrous gift in these last few months of the year.

Lisa Cherrett

The Messy Nativity project

Jane Leadbetter

Liverpool 2009: there were robins, snowmen, baubles, penguins and Christmas decorations in the city shops. Santa's Grotto bookings were high and new ways of celebrating the season with the family were everywhere, such as giant snow globes to climb into and have a photo taken, or ice rinks popping up in shopping malls where people could skate with Santa and his elves. There were the inevitable pantomimes and Winterfests advertised in the local paper.

So why was I feeling pricklier than Christmas holly this particular year? Because I couldn't find Jesus anywhere as I shopped for Christmas presents. The feeling of consternation stayed with me for a long time until I knew that I had to have a go at doing something about it, no matter how small.

Before working for BRF, I was the Children's Work Adviser for the Diocese of Liverpool. I enjoyed working in collaboration with many Christian organisations, and this Advent I found myself talking with the Liverpool Mothers' Union. Some of their members recalled the Posada activity, in which nativity sets are passed around the homes of church families during Advent, recreating the journey of Mary and Joseph. I also remembered the knitting patterns for nativity characters in the Diocesan Resources Room.

Liverpool is well known for its trails. In the recent past we have had a hugely successful 'Superlambanana' trail around the city, followed by 'Penguins Go!' Families love hunting for decorated models and trying to complete the trails before their friends. With all of this in mind, I was praying about finding local community activities that could be easily prepared, were lots of fun and would bring Jesus back into Christmas in our cities, towns and villages. So, in 2009, a Messy Nativity project began.

The project began with requests for knitters to find knitting patterns for sheep in particular. The MU was very good at hunting down tried-and-tested patterns and, after also looking on the internet, we prepared a pack of suggested sheep patterns. My own daughter created a large version of a knitted sheep and people all over Merseyside began knitting small and large sheep. My life began to change in most unexpected ways. Sheep appeared on my porch, in my car boot and on my desk, and they came in a variety of shapes and colours. Some even had names. Messy sheep seemed to be loved by all ages.

With the Liverpool MU we started Part One of a three-part project for Advent 2010, encouraging parishes to choose a nativity set to pass around the homes in their community, along with knitted sheep. As each home passed the nativity set on to the next, they kept back a small knitted sheep as a reminder of the story. Ideas for a church service or sheep event were shared to bring the community together to experience the real Christmas story. Some Christingle services focused on the sheep and shepherds.

> ***At last we had Jesus back in town!***

Part Two of the Messy Nativity project involved placing slightly larger knitted sheep in stores in Liverpool ONE, the city's major shopping and leisure centre. Remembering the trail culture of Merseyside families, I embarked on creating a sheep trail. I gained permission from retail management to ask twelve shops, including GAP, Debenhams, Waterstone's and John Lewis, if I could place a large knitted sheep inside their store. Each store chose where to place the sheep—on counters, on shelving or on the Christmas tree—and they were decorated with tinsel and Christmas bells. Each store was asked to name their sheep for a competition: we had Berry, Bauble, Angel, Dolly, Frank, Don, Kevin, Sheila, Purl, Bertie, Timmy Time and Horace. I promised I would not ask the shop staff to take on any more work, but alongside each sheep would be a pile of sheep trail leaflets. When families had found all the sheep and completed the front of the leaflet with the names, they could take part in a prize draw during Christmas week. Some of the participating stores offered voucher prizes. The rest of the leaflet contained text of the nativity story to take home. At last we had Jesus back in town!

The shops loved the idea, quickly recognising the trail's potential to increase footfall and create a sense of theatre for shoppers. The trail also captured the imagination of local radio and newspaper reporters, who helped to advertise the project. Afterwards, I found some shops very reluctant to give back their sheep, as they had become part of the fixtures and fittings, and I received requests for an Easter trail. Who would have thought that knitted sheep could become so popular with all ages?

Part Three of the project was nearly scuppered by bad weather—nearly! The idea was that, if Jesus was being introduced into homes in local communities and through the nativity story on the trail leaflets, we needed to dramatise the nativity story in the street to passers-by, to help people of all ages realise that Christmas was all about celebrating the birth of Jesus. For this part of the project, I approached a handful of volunteers and we hunted for suitable scripts and props. At this time I was contacted by a chaplain at the city centre indoor market. Could we put on the drama in the market during Christmas week? Perhaps move around, repeating it, and involving the audience—traders, passers-by and so on? What an exciting challenge! The city centre precinct manager heard about it too and invited us to perform the nativity story on the pavements outside. So we had our authorised venues.

We found a simple script that allowed the addition of Christmas carols after each nativity character had been introduced. I ordered small Christmas tracts to give out, and the MU joined us and gave out copies of their *Families First* magazines. Despite the snowfall, we all managed to turn up and had fun performing and encouraging others to be angels and shepherds. On the Saturday we performed the nativity story in four different locations—and we gave out knitted sheep.

> ***It is worth doing something rather than nothing***

Since the completion of the Messy Nativity project 2010, I have been contacted by people from all over the country, asking for sheep knitting patterns and help with organising various parts of the project. Cities, shopping malls, towns and villages, north and south of Liverpool, put on their own versions of the project during Advent 2011.

If you would like to do something similar, see page 146 for details of a book to help you. The project can be easily split into three parts. You may feel God asking you just to do one part of the project, but, whatever you choose, remember that it is worth doing something rather than nothing in our present social climate. You may think that you can't make much impact, but just a few key people can make all the difference. Presenting the best story ever told to people who have never heard it is so important. More and more people are oblivious as to why we celebrate Christmas. I believe we need to go into the streets and community at Christmas, where the people are living their busy and messy lives. Come and join in with the mess!

Jane Leadbetter is a member of the BRF Messy Church team.

Barnabas Children's Ministry

Martyn Payne

To my astonishment, 2012 sees me completing ten years with BRF as part of the Barnabas Children's Ministry team—and what an amazing decade it has been! Our face-to-face work with teachers and children in primary schools has grown hugely since I started. Now, for most of the weeks of any given term, the team is in action every day in at least two schools nationally. This is a cause for great praise to God, who has definitely been inspiring and guiding us each step of the way in answer to your faithful prayers and encouragement as BRF readers. Thank you!

Equally exciting has been the growth of our work with churches. This includes both the incredible national and international enthusiasm for a fresh expression of church for children and families in the shape of Messy Church and the existence of our highly respected website for children's leaders and ministers. Many people regularly turn to it for ideas on how to bring the Bible to life for all ages. Put alongside all this our published resources (which continue to receive positive reviews from all quarters) and we clearly have so much to be thankful for.

I have been privileged to be a small part of this phenomenal growth over my ten years with BRF and I am constantly amazed at how God has led me and has blessed our Barnabas work. I hope you too are excited about what is happening and eager to see where God is leading us next.

Looking back, one of the reasons why Barnabas Children's Ministry continues to be so successful is, I believe, that we have been listening closely to what the Spirit of God is saying to the churches about mission among children and families in particular. There is no doubt that children's work through churches is changing, and these changes often demand that we use new approaches and resources, while holding on to our calling to open up the Bible thoughtfully and creatively, which has been at the core of BRF's vision throughout its 90 years.

Our listening has meant that we have embraced and, we hope, contributed to important influences over this ten-year period, such as insights from Godly Play™ as well as the challenge to present Christian truths attractively and faithfully within an educational setting. Our playful, explorative and interactive approach to the Bible has won many friends among teachers, and this same approach seems to meet with the most success in churches, too. It is a methodology that both respects the spirituality of children and gives them space to make their own discoveries about our faith. A mantra of ours has been simply this: that, as we open up the Bible creatively, we can trust this inspired word and the inspiration of the Holy Spirit to inspire children on their own spiritual journey.

Another way in which the Barnabas Children's Ministry team has been listening to God's Spirit can be seen in our passion for Bible storytelling, which has been just right for this day and age. Live storytelling is back in fashion, particularly for a generation that, I believe, welcomes any break from the ever-present image on a screen. We see children's faces light up when they are invited to hear and become part of a story, in which their imaginations can be set free and, most importantly, they can hear God speaking for themselves. Our writing-free, screen-free and worksheet-free approach to sharing the Bible has so much to commend it. This inclusive and interactive way of exploring the great truths of the Gospel is, I believe, much more likely to take root, and it has become a distinctive hallmark of the way our Barnabas team works.

As we look ahead to the next ten years, however, it is clear that we will need to keep listening to God, to discern where he is leading us. For example, we can already sense that much traditional Sunday group work is in decline and that, in its place, a whole-family approach is needed—as made evident by the growth of Messy Church and our new initiative for supporting faith development during the week in the home environment. Put alongside this the increased interest from many churches in how to make true whole-community worship and learning work well—in a way that offers a truly radical intergenerational template for supporting each other on a shared, all-age spiritual journey—and the next ten years look to be as exciting as the last.

I hope you are as thrilled as I am to see what God is doing through BRF on so many fronts. In fact, I believe that we are being as revolutionary today as our founder was at BRF's beginnings, when his first Bible notes began rolling off the St Matthew's printing press 90 years ago. I am so glad that I have been part of this particular adventure. Please join me in waiting eagerly and praying faithfully for the next instalment.

Martyn Payne is a member of the Barnabas Children's Ministry team, based in the south-east of England.

Recommended reading

We may sometimes feel that we're over-familiar with the Gospel stories, especially the Advent and Christmas narratives—so it is always helpful to find new insights and creative ways of learning and teaching these stories. Our 'Recommended reading' in this issue highlights four books that will inspire you to take a fresh look at biblical events and characters, with a special emphasis on ideas for the Advent and Christmas season.

Messy Nativity
How to run your very own Messy Nativity Advent project
Jane Leadbetter

On pages 141–143, Messy Church team member Jane Leadbetter writes about the success of the all-age Messy Nativity Sheep Trail at twelve leading stores in the heart of Liverpool's city centre. The success in Liverpool demonstrates that UK city centres are interested in new and fun ways to attract customers and offer them an experience they will not find online. To help you get involved in your area, BRF is now delighted to announce the publication of *Messy Nativity: How to run your very own Messy Nativity Advent project*. Written by Jane, the book provides all you need to know to set up your own nativity trail and more. Why not order your copy now and join other churches that are bringing Jesus back into Christmas for shoppers across the country?
ISBN 978 0 85746 055 4, pb, 64 pages, £5.99

Messy Christmas Crafts
A treasure trove of Advent, Christmas and Epiphany ideas for Messy Churches
Lucy Moore and Jane Leadbetter

Building on the popularity of *Messy Crafts*, this book extends the range of excitingly messy activities with a particular focus on the Christmas season. There are three complete sessions for Advent, Christmas and Epiphany, together with creative Christmas prayers, global action sug-

gestions, games and competitions, Christmas food crafts and many other ideas to take you on into the New Year.
ISBN 978 0 85746 091 2, pb, 96 pages, £5.99

Jesus: Name Above All Names
32 Bible studies on the person and work of Jesus
Anne Le Tissier

Anne offers straightforward, devotionally based Bible study material on 32 names and titles ascribed to Jesus in scripture. From 'Advocate' to 'Word of God', the studies consider what we can learn about who Jesus is and what he has done for us from the different names and titles. The material also includes questions for response, prayers and suggestions for further Bible reading.

Prepared from articles originally published in *Woman Alive* magazine, which is celebrating its 30th birthday this year.
ISBN 978 0 85746 085 1, pb, 240 pages, £7.99

Walking with Gospel Women
Bible-based meditations
Fiona Stratta

Twenty-five reflective monologues drawing on the voices and stories of women who appear in the Gospel narratives. The approach used is inspired by Ignatian spirituality—imaginatively putting yourself in the context of a particular story (especially one that may already be very familiar) in order to draw out fresh lessons for today. The monologues cover the events of the Gospels, starting with Elizabeth and the annunciation to Mary, and concluding with Mary Magdalene's encounter with the risen Jesus.

The introduction explains how to use the book, including how to facilitate group use.
ISBN 978 0 85746 010 3, pb, 168 pages, £6.99

To order a copy of any of these books, please turn to the order form on page 153, or visit www.brfonline.org.uk.

An extract from *Companions on the Bethlehem Road*

This book of daily Bible readings and reflections for Advent and Christmas is based around spiritual insights gleaned from some of the best-loved poets of the past—Eliot, Herbert, Tennyson and Auden, among others. This book is not a literary study of their work but a quest to see what they can tell us about life and faith today. Their poems are quoted in short sections, with suggestions about what they might mean for us now. The following abridged extract is taken from the Introduction to the book.

What poets can show us

I want to suggest that poetry can be enormously helpful in our journey of faith. The poets' finely honed words have much to say to us, right now. They might come from very different ages and backgrounds, but they faced the same questions that we do—about God, human love and the problem of suffering, for example. They have often thought about these questions more deeply than most of us do, and their works endure because the fruit of their reflection still speaks vividly to so many of us…

For it often seems that it is only in poetry that our deepest yearnings can come to the surface. There are so many aspects of God's love for us and ours for him that are hard, if not impossible, to grasp that we can only catch glimpses of part of the picture. The tangential nature of poems—coming at our experience from a particular angle, not feeling they need to record it exhaustively—means that they are ideally placed to convey the complexity, delight and glory of God's care for his creation.

The New Zealand poet James K. Baxter (1926–72) refers to 'an attitude of listening out of which poems may arise… the unheard sound of which poems are translations'. We can make some headway in analysing this attitude but, in the end, it can never be pinned down. God is with us and in us, but also always beyond us. He created us but he doesn't need us; his creation is pure gift.

Poems, which go beyond a merely literal description of the world, hint at this unknowability, this state of reaching towards infinity. As the French poet Paul Valéry (1871–1945) noted, 'A poem is never finished, only abandoned.' Poets are content to explore and deepen the mystery of God, rather than being obsessed with resolving it. So, for example, several poets whom I quote tease out the paradoxes of Jesus' coming from his heavenly kingdom to be born as a defenceless baby—for instance, John Donne (1572–1631) in 'Annunciation' and 'Nativity': 'Immensity cloistered in thy dear womb' (see the readings for 20 December and Christmas Day). They are not studying this paradox as a problem to be explained so much as a mystery to be revelled in…

Advent themes

Advent—the four-and-a-bit weeks before Christmas—is more than just a preparation for the festive season. It is a distinctive time in the Church's year, with its own features, which are a rich blend of different themes. Like Lent, it is a time of penitence, a time to prepare ourselves inwardly for a great festival at its end by reconsidering where we have fallen short. In this respect, it offers a wonderful chance to examine ourselves, to review our lives in a way that we seldom bother to do. We can try to look at ourselves honestly, to probe our sins and repent of them.

Poets are content to explore… the mystery of God

It forms a fascinating interplay with the secular calendar. Advent, the beginning of the Church's year, is when we look both backwards and forwards—just as the secular world does at its New Year, although it concentrates that mood in the few days around 1 January. But, much more than this, the special themes of Advent give it a unique focus, and one that is all too rare for most of us to think about now: death and judgment. The traditional concerns of the four weeks of the season are death, judgment, heaven and hell. This focus also links with the way that, as part of our preparation for the first coming of Jesus at Christmas, churches have traditionally considered its connections with the second coming at the end of time. We look at how the people of God have prepared for this—through the patriarchs and prophets, and on to those directly involved in the events of the nativity: John the Baptist and Mary.

Part of our preparation today involves us in self-examination and penitence, which are sharpened up by our sense of our ultimate end. No matter that most of us manage to put off all thoughts of the end—usually until death becomes an immediate prospect. This season presents a unique opportunity to think about what ultimately matters. It need not be gloomy: the judgment of God offers redemption for the wrongs we have suffered. In the Old Testament, the poor of Israel look forward to it eagerly, as the time when they will be vindicated. Advent Bible readings refer to this redemption specifically: for example, Zechariah's song for his son, John the Baptist, says, 'Blessed be the Lord God of Israel: for he hath visited and redeemed his people' (Luke 1:68: see the reading for Christmas Eve).

During the weeks of Advent, we will be considering these themes but then moving on to ideas about Christmas. Not surprisingly, another part of the point of Advent is to think over Christmas itself, the coming of God into our world—Jesus' becoming one of us and taking on our flesh in the incarnation. The implications of this are staggering, and it should take a lifetime to ponder them. To take just one example, it means that God loves every aspect of our world (as John 3:16 suggests). Jesus entered fully into our humanity; he didn't just visit briefly or dip in his toe. He was not like the Ancient Greek gods who popped down to earth, mainly to cause trouble. Also, we often hear about how incarnational theology should influence our attitude to our planet and to our fellow creatures, human and animal. If God loves the world he has made enough to come and be part of it, we too should cherish it and the other creatures in it. So Advent isn't just about our soul and inner peace: we are only one small part of his whole creation, all under the rule of God into eternity.

About this book

The readings are all drawn from the lectionary, the official pattern of Bible passages set down by the Church for its daily worship. This means that we will always be reading verses alongside other Christians, even if we are on our own. It can be very moving to think that thousands of others are pondering the same parts of scripture, as well as to know that the passages have been specially chosen for this day in the year as part of a carefully thought-out plan to cover the most important aspects of our faith.

The book runs all the way through Advent and the beginning of the Christmas season, right up to the Epiphany on 6 January. Its readings can be used in any year, although the book was first written with Advent 2012 in mind.

To order a copy of this book, please turn to the order form on page 153, or visit www.brfonline.org.uk.

SUPPORTING BRF'S MINISTRY

As a Christian charity, BRF is involved in five distinct yet complementary areas.

- BRF (www.brf.org.uk) resources adults for their spiritual journey through Bible reading notes, books, and a programme of quiet days and teaching days. BRF also provides the infrastructure that supports our other four specialist ministries.
- **Foundations21** (www.foundations21.org.uk) provides flexible and innovative ways for individuals and groups to explore their Christian faith and discipleship through a multimedia internet-based resource.
- **Messy Church** (www.messychurch.org.uk), led by Lucy Moore, enables churches all over the UK (and increasingly abroad) to reach children and adults beyond the fringes of the church .
- **Barnabas in Churches** (www.barnabasinchurches.org.uk) helps churches to support, resource and develop their children's ministry with the under-11s more effectively .
- **Barnabas in Schools** (www.barnabasinschools.org.uk) enables primary school children and teachers to explore Christianity creatively and bring the Bible alive within RE and Collective Worship.

At the heart of BRF's ministry is a desire to equip adults and children for Christian living—helping them to read and understand the Bible, to explore prayer and to grow as disciples of Jesus. We need your help to make a real impact on the local church, local schools and the wider community.

- You could support BRF's ministry with a donation or standing order (using the response form overleaf).
- You could consider making a bequest to BRF in your will.
- You could encourage your church to support BRF as part of your church's giving to home mission—perhaps focusing on a specific area of our ministry, or a particular member of our Barnabas team.
- Most important of all, you could support BRF with your prayers.

If you would like to discuss how a specific gift or bequest could be used in the development of our ministry, please phone 01865 319700 or email enquiries@brf.org.uk.

Whatever you can do or give, we thank you for your support.

BRF MINISTRY APPEAL RESPONSE FORM

Name ______________________________

Address ______________________________

______________________________ Postcode __________

Telephone ______________ Email ______________

Gift Aid Declaration

❑ I am a UK taxpayer. I want BRF to treat as Gift Aid Donations all donations I make from 6 April 2000 until I notify you otherwise.

Signature ______________________________ Date __________

❑ I would like to support BRF's ministry with a regular donation by standing order

Standing Order – Banker's Order

To the Manager, Name of Bank/Building Society

Address ______________________________

______________________________ Postcode __________

Sort Code ______________ Account Name ______________

Account No ______________________________

Please pay Royal Bank of Scotland plc, Drummonds, 49 Charing Cross, London SW1A 2DX (Sort Code 16-00-38), for the account of BRF A/C No. 00774151

The sum of _____ pounds on ___/___ /___ (insert date) and thereafter the same amount on the same day each month / same day annually (delete as applic.) until further notice.

Signature ______________________________ Date __________

Single donation

❑ I enclose my cheque/credit card/Switch card details for a donation of £5 £10 £25 £50 £100 £250 (other) £ _____ to support BRF's ministry

Card no. | | | | | | | | | | | | | | | | |

Expires | | | | | **Security code** | | | | **Issue no.** | | | |

Signature ______________________________ Date __________

Please use my donation for ❑ BRF ❑ Foundations21 ❑ Messy Church ❑ Barnabas for Children

❑ Please send me information about making a bequest to BRF in my will.

Please detach and send this completed form to: Richard Fisher, BRF, 15 The Chambers, Vineyard, Abingdon OX14 3FE. BRF is a Registered Charity (No.233280)

BRF PUBLICATIONS ORDER FORM

Please ensure that you complete and send off both sides of this order form.

Please send me the following book(s):		Quantity	Price	Total
065 3	Companions on the Bethlehem Road (*R. Boulding*)	______	£7.99	______
085 1	Jesus: Name Above All Names (*A. Le Tissier*)	______	£7.99	______
010 3	Walking with Gospel Women (*F. Stratta*)	______	£6.99	______
055 4	Messy Nativity (*J. Leadbetter*)	______	£5.99	______
091 2	Messy Christmas Crafts (*L.Moore & J. Leadbetter*)	______	£5.99	______
063 9	Family Fun for Christmas (*J. Butcher*)	______	£4.99	______

Total cost of books £ ________

Donation £ ________

Postage and packing £ ________

TOTAL £ ________

POSTAGE AND PACKING CHARGES				
order value	UK	Europe	Surface	Air Mail
£7.00 & under	£1.25	£3.00	£3.50	£5.50
£7.01–£30.00	£2.25	£5.50	£6.50	£10.00
Over £30.00	free	prices on request		

For more information about new books and special offers, visit www.brfonline.org.uk.

See over for payment details.

All prices are correct at time of going to press, are subject to the prevailing rate of VAT and may be subject to change without prior warning.

PAYMENT DETAILS

WAYS TO ORDER BRF RESOURCES

Christian bookshops: All good Christian bookshops stock BRF publications. For your nearest stockist, please contact BRF.

Telephone: The BRF office is open between 09.15 and 17.30. To place your order, phone 01865 319700; fax 01865 319701.

Web: Visit www.brfonline.org.uk

By post: Please complete the payment details below and send with appropriate payment and completed order form to:

BRF, 15 The Chambers, Vineyard, Abingdon OX14 3FE

Name ______________________________

Address ______________________________

______________________________ Postcode ____________

Telephone ______________________________

Email ______________________________

Total enclosed £____________ (cheques should be made payable to 'BRF')

Please charge my Visa ❑ Mastercard ❑ Switch card ❑ with £__________

Card no: ☐☐☐☐☐☐☐☐☐☐☐☐☐☐☐☐

Expires ☐☐☐☐ **Security code** ☐☐☐

Issue no (Switch only) ☐☐☐☐

Signature (essential if paying by credit/Switch) ______________________________

❑ Please do not send me further information about BRF publications.

BRF is a Registered Charity

BIBLE READING RESOURCES PACK

Thank you for reading BRF Bible reading notes. BRF has been producing a variety of Bible reading notes for over 90 years, helping people all over the UK and the world connect with the Bible on a personal level every day.

Could you help us find other people who would enjoy our notes?

We produce a Bible Reading Resource Pack for church groups to use to encourage regular Bible reading.

This FREE pack contains:

- Samples of all BRF Bible reading notes.
- Our Resources for Personal Bible Reading catalogue, providing all you need to know about our Bible reading notes.
- A ready-to-use church magazine feature about BRF notes.
- Ready-made sermon and all-age service ideas to help your church into the Bible (ideal for Bible Sunday events).
- And much more!

How to order your FREE pack:

- Visit: www.biblereadingnotes.org.uk/request-a-bible-reading-resources-pack/
- Telephone: 01865 319700
- Post: Complete the form below and post to: Bible Reading Resource Pack, BRF, 15 The Chambers, Vineyard, Abingdon, OX14 3FE

Name ________________________________

Address ________________________________

____

____________________ Postcode ________

Telephone ________________________________

Email ________________________________

Please send me ________ Bible Reading Resources Pack(s)

This pack is produced free of charge for all UK addresses but, if you wish to offer a donation towards our costs, this would be appreciated. If you require a pack to be sent outside of the UK, please contact us for details of postage and packing charges. Tel: +44 1865 319700. Thank you.

BRF is a Registered Charity

NEW DAYLIGHT INDIVIDUAL SUBSCRIPTIONS

❑ I would like to take out a subscription myself:

Your name ______________________________

Your address ______________________________

____

______________________________ Postcode __________

Tel ______________ Email ______________________________

Please send *New Daylight* beginning with the January 2013 / May 2013 / September 2013 issue: (delete as applicable)

(please tick box)	UK	SURFACE	AIR MAIL
NEW DAYLIGHT	❑ £15.00	❑ £17.10	❑ £20.25
NEW DAYLIGHT 3-year sub	❑ £37.80		
NEW DAYLIGHT DELUXE	❑ £18.99	❑ £24.60	❑ £31.50
NEW DAYLIGHT daily email only	❑ £12.00 (UK and overseas)		

Please complete the payment details below and send with appropriate payment to: **BRF, 15 The Chambers, Vineyard, Abingdon OX14 3FE**

Total enclosed £ __________ (cheques should be made payable to 'BRF')

Please charge my Visa ❑ Mastercard ❑ Switch card ❑ with £

Card no: ☐☐☐☐☐☐☐☐☐☐☐☐☐☐☐☐

Expires ☐☐☐☐ Security code ☐☐☐

Issue no (Switch only) ☐☐☐☐

Signature (essential if paying by card) ______________________________

To set up a direct debit, please also complete the form on page 159 and send it to BRF with this form.

BRF is a Registered Charity

NEW DAYLIGHT GIFT SUBSCRIPTIONS

❏ I would like to give a gift subscription (please provide both names and addresses:

Your name ______________________________

Your address ______________________________

______________________________ Postcode ____________

Tel ______________ Email ______________________________

Gift subscription name ______________________________

Gift subscription address ______________________________

______________________________ Postcode ____________

Gift message (20 words max. or include your own gift card for the recipient)

____

____

Please send *New Daylight* beginning with the January 2013 / May 2013 / September 2013 issue: (delete as applicable)

(please tick box)	UK	SURFACE	AIR MAIL
NEW DAYLIGHT	❏ £15.00	❏ £17.10	❏ £20.25
NEW DAYLIGHT 3-year sub	❏ £37.80		
NEW DAYLIGHT DELUXE	❏ £18.99	❏ £24.60	❏ £31.50
NEW DAYLIGHT daily email only	❏ £12.00 (UK and overseas)		

Please complete the payment details below and send with appropriate payment to: **BRF, 15 The Chambers, Vineyard, Abingdon OX14 3FE**

Total enclosed £ ____________ (cheques should be made payable to 'BRF')

Please charge my Visa ❏ Mastercard ❏ Switch card ❏ with £

Card no: ☐☐☐☐☐☐☐☐☐☐☐☐☐☐☐☐

Expires ☐☐☐☐ **Security code** ☐☐☐

Issue no (Switch only) ☐☐☐☐

Signature (essential if paying by card) ______________________________

To set up a direct debit, please also complete the form on page 159 and send it to BRF with this form.

DIRECT DEBIT PAYMENTS

Now you can pay for your annual subscription to BRF notes using Direct Debit. You need only give your bank details once, and the payment is made automatically every year until you cancel it. If you would like to pay by Direct Debit, please use the form opposite, entering your BRF account number under 'Reference'.

You are fully covered by the Direct Debit Guarantee:

The Direct Debit Guarantee

DIRECT Debit

- This Guarantee is offered by all banks and building societies that accept instructions to pay Direct Debits.
- If there are any changes to the amount, date or frequency of your Direct Debit, The Bible Reading Fellowship will notify you 10 working days in advance of your account being debited or as otherwise agreed. If you request The Bible Reading Fellowship to collect a payment, confirmation of the amount and date will be given to you at the time of the request.
- If an error is made in the payment of your Direct Debit, by The Bible Reading Fellowship or your bank or building society, you are entitled to a full and immediate refund of the amount paid from your bank or building society.
  - – If you receive a refund you are not entitled to, you must pay it back when The Bible Reading Fellowship asks you to.
- You can cancel a Direct Debit at any time by simply contacting your bank or building society. Written confirmation may be required. Please also notify us.

The Bible Reading Fellowship

Instruction to your bank or building society to pay by Direct Debit

Please fill in the whole form using a ballpoint pen and send to The Bible Reading Fellowship, 15 The Chambers, Vineyard, Abingdon OX14 3FE.

Service User Number: | 5 | 5 | 8 | 2 | 2 | 9 |

Name and full postal address of your bank or building society

To: The Manager Bank/Building Society

Address

Postcode

Name(s) of account holder(s)

Branch sort code

Bank/Building Society account number

Reference

Instruction to your Bank/Building Society

Please pay The Bible Reading Fellowship Direct Debits from the account detailed in this instruction, subject to the safeguards assured by the Direct Debit Guarantee.
I understand that this instruction may remain with The Bible Reading Fellowship and, if so, details will be passed electronically to my bank/building society.

Signature(s)

Date

Banks and Building Societies may not accept Direct Debit instructions for some types of account.

This page is intentionally left blank.